The Political Economy of East Asia

Series editors
Ming Wan
Vienna, Virginia, USA

Natasha Hamilton-Hart
The University of Auckland Business School
Auckland, New Zealand

The Political Economy of East Asia publishes high-quality, innovative research on the political economies of Northeast Asia and Southeast Asia. Covering both comparative political economy and international political economy, the series showcases research that explores the diversity of national trajectories, as well as the linkages that connect these countries to regional and global economies. The Political Economy of East Asia promotes theoretically-informed scholarship that investigates issues of contemporary social, political and economic importance. The series seeks to contribute to increased understanding of East Asia, both as a major center of global economic growth and as a region facing critical challenges that lie at the intersection of politics and economics. This series seeks to promote pluralistic debate on topics including, but not limited to: monetary policy, economic reform, shared growth, production networks, regionalism, agribusiness, consumer protection, and labor politics.

More information about this series at
http://www.springer.com/series/14416

Joel David Moore

Varieties of Capitalism in Southeast Asia

palgrave
macmillan

Joel David Moore
Monash University Malaysia
Bandar Sunway, Malaysia

The Political Economy of East Asia
ISBN 978-3-319-53699-6 ISBN 978-3-319-53700-9 (eBook)
DOI 10.1007/978-3-319-53700-9

Library of Congress Control Number: 2017939550

Printed on acid-free paper

This Palgrave Macmillan imprint is published by Springer Nature
The registered company is Springer International Publishing AG
The registered company address is: Gewerbestrasse 11, 6330 Cham, Switzerland

Contents

1	Capitalist Varieties: An Introduction	1
2	Constraints and Development	9
3	Thailand: From Autocrats to Oversized Coalitions	33
4	Malaysia: Thriving Under Neglect	105
5	Singapore: Constraints and Coordination	149
6	Comparisons and Conclusions	161
Bibliography		173
Index		175

List of Figures

Fig. 1.1	Varieties of capitalism and the impact of veto players	4
Fig. 2.1	Typological framework	16
Fig. 2.2	Firm structure under liberal corporate governance systems	23
Fig. 2.3	Firm structure under coordinated corporate governance systems	24
Fig. 2.4	Firm structure under hierarchical corporate governance systems	24
Fig. 3.1	World crude oil prices (inflation adjusted USD)	49
Fig. 4.1	Value of primary commodity exports in Malaysia (1964–1969)	109
Fig. 4.2	Value of primary commodity exports in Malaysia (1970–1989)	116
Fig. 4.3	Value of resource exports in Malaysia (1989–2014)	116
Fig. 4.4	Malaysian government deficit (1970–1989)	119
Fig. 4.5	Malaysian government deficit (1990–2008)	119
Fig. 4.6	Control of corruption in Malaysia	124
Fig. 4.7	Malaysian federal development expenditures per capita by state	134
Fig. 6.1	Expectations and findings for the policy environment	162

List of Tables

Table 2.1	Case selection	17
Table 3.1	Observations in the Thai case	34
Table 3.2	BoI promotion in the electronics industry	44
Table 3.3	Family firm JV partners in the early electrical industry	45
Table 3.4	US assistance to Thailand US Aid and Military Assistance in millions of US Dollars	48
Table 3.5	BoT rediscounting credit for the electronics industry	51
Table 3.6	Size of coalition governments in the coalition democracy period	67
Table 3.7	Firm ownership in Thailand (1996)	73
Table 3.8	Size of Coalition Governments in the Post-Crisis Period	78
Table 3.9	Thai commercial banks before and after the asian crisis in 1997	82
Table 3.10	Change in ownership and control after the crisis	84
Table 3.11	Percentage of shares held by top ten shareholders	90
Table 3.12	Constraints, policy environment, and economic governance institutions in Thailand	93
Table 4.1	Vulnerability and number of veto players in Malaysia and Penang	106
Table 4.2	Malay electoral advantage in peninsular Malaysia	110
Table 4.3	Peninsular Malaysia: Ownership of share capital	112
Table 4.4	Ordinary shareholdings by types of Malaysian financial companies	113
Table 4.5	Old vs. New Chinese firms	128
Table 4.6	Estimated distribution of firm by size in PDC industrial areas	138

CHAPTER 1

Capitalist Varieties: An Introduction

At the start of the 1980s, Kulthorn Engineering, a Thai air conditioning import company, sat down with the world's most important electrical appliance producers, the Thai government, and some of Thailand's most powerful business families. Together, they created and implemented a plan to develop the local capacity to produce high value-added refrigeration and air-conditioning components in Thailand using the world's latest technologies. Facilitated by one of the many newly established peak business associations in the country, the strong network that arose around Kulthorn featured intensive cooperation and led directly to the emergence of Thailand as the world's second largest air conditioner and refrigerator manufacturer in 2005.[1] It was one of the several stunning examples in the 1980s of a dense production network of local and multinational firms coordinating their efforts to overcome major market failures.

Unfortunately, the rapid expansion of coordinative networks did not last and the 1990s were marked by the rise of electronics conglomerates like Alphatec, which thrived for a time because of powerful patrons rather than deep coordination in the industry. In the mid-2000s, Kulthorn again attempted an ambitious move to get local appliance producers to work together to establish a Thai brand in the sector. The effort, which would have further increased the value added to local companies, fizzled as the decade progressed. Why has coordination in the Thai electronics industry been so uneven over time? If intensive coordination had been so instrumental in facilitating rapid advancement in the sector, why was it not replicated in later periods?

J.D. Moore, *Varieties of Capitalism in Southeast Asia*, The Political Economy of East Asia, DOI 10.1007/978-3-319-53700-9_1

Another puzzling case of failing to replicate successful coordination is evident in Malaysia. From the 1970s through the mid-1990s, local electrical producers in Penang such as Eng Hardware and LKT Engineering rapidly climbed up the value chain by pooling knowledge and capacities and working closely with multinational lead firms, like Intel. While electronics producers in other Malaysian states were encouraged to participate in coordinative institutions that were designed to mimic those in Penang, meaningful coordination did not occur. Why did these attempts fail in Malaysia's other states despite a clear model and active promotion? What was the missing ingredient? The lack of sustained, countrywide coordination in Thailand and Malaysia is even more puzzling considering the tremendous gains that were achieved in Singapore, where coordination between local and multinational electronics firms was the most extensive.

Why do some of the most fundamental firm characteristics—the roles played by their owners and financers, the relations they have with their customers and suppliers, and the sorts of skills their employees possess and develop—vary from country to country and period to period? What explains why governance institutions have evolved so differently around the world? Unfortunately, there is a considerable disconnect between the importance of these questions and the development of theories offered to answer them. This book employs a modified version of the VoC framework to conceptualize the differences between developing economic systems and to explore their determinants in a systematic way.

The VoC literature characterizes the tremendous diversity of national economic governance institutions, the rules and dominant practices that structure interactions between workers, managers, and investors in an economy (Hall and Soskice 2001; Gourevitch 2003; Gourevitch and Hawes 2002; Gourevitch and Shinn 2005). These institutions structure whether firms have access to quickly raised financing that demands immediate profits or depend on more patient investors that are willing to pursue investments with longer term returns. They determine whether firms have institutionalized relations with employees that prohibit mass layoffs but enable the provision of industry-specific skills or can easily shed unskilled workers as is necessary. They also shape the relations that firms have with their competitors and suppliers; in some cases facilitating intensive information sharing and cooperation and in others allowing only arms-length transactions.

The VoC approach provides a framework for making sense of patterns of economic activity and innovation across the developed world (Hall and Soskice 2001). In this approach, scholars contrast two ideal type economic governance systems: liberal market economies (LME) such as the United States with coordinated market economies (CME) like Germany. Specific types of economic governance institutions tend to bunch together because of complementary features, leading to integrated systems that maximize either flexibility and adaptability or deep cooperation. In LMEs, economic governance institutions unleash the full creative and destructive powers of the market. Fierce competition dominates among firms that maintain arm's length transactions and have access to fluid labor and capital markets. In contrast, CMEs have a range of market-supporting institutions that facilitate dense coordination among firms, investors, and workers. Each is thought to provide actors within its boundaries a comparative advantage in different innovational and economic activities (Hall and Soskice 2001).

Institutions in individual countries should tend to cluster about these two ideal-types, which feature a bundle of complementary economic governance institutions.[2] The VoC literature identifies five such institutions: (1) industrial relations, (2) corporate governance, (3) worker training, (4) inter-firm relations, and (5) firm structure. Industrial relations structure the relationship between firms and workers, featuring strong, centralized unions in CMEs and weak, decentralized unions in LMEs. Corporate governance institutions structure the relationship between firms and investors, featuring patient bank lending or cross-shareholding in CMEs and fluid, diffuse capital investments in LMEs. Worker training institutions determine the sorts of skills that workers develop, featuring industry-specific skills in CMEs and general skills in LMEs. Inter-firm relations structure the relationships among firms horizontally and vertically, featuring strong cooperative relationships among firms in CMEs and arms-length interactions among firms in LMEs. The structure of the firm also varies between the two, with broad participation decision-making by workers, owners, and management in CMEs and independent, hierarchically controlled management in LMEs. Together these institutions influence such important outputs as wage levels, shareholder concentration, and innovation patterns.[3]

One reason that these institutions are expected to cluster is that institutions of the same class are thought to be complementary. That is, each coordinative (liberal) governance institution will increase the returns to all the other coordinative (liberal) governance institutions in that country. For example, having a coordinative corporate governance institution should reduce the threat that agreements with workers, competitors, or suppliers will be either prevented by investors interested in short-run profitability or undermined in the future by a hostile takeover. While the primary objects of study in the VoC literature are the economic and innovational outcomes of governance institutions, several of these scholars also consider the origins of these economy types.

Though Hall and Soskice were more focused on characterizing these systems, they did suggest that the frequency of radical policy change might explain why different systems developed in different countries. When governments are constrained from radically altering economic policies, workers, managers, and investors ought to feel less inhibited from acquiring and holding co-specific assets. Co-specific assets are investments whose value depends on the active participation of other actors and which cannot be easily switched to another use. Examples include research and development consortia and industry-specific training centers. Subsequent work has done more to explicitly examine and test this possibility. Research by Gourevitch and others has found support for the argument that the number of veto players, actors whose assent is required before policies may be changed, influences the type of economic institutions that develop by making the policy environment more or less stable.[4]

More specifically, there should be a positive relationship between the number of veto players in a country and the degree to which they have a stable policy environment and coordinative governance institutions (Hall and Soskice 2001, 49). Figure 1.1 shows the expected relationship graphically. As the number of veto players increases, investors, managers, and workers become more willing to hold co-specific assets and form coordinated governance institutions.

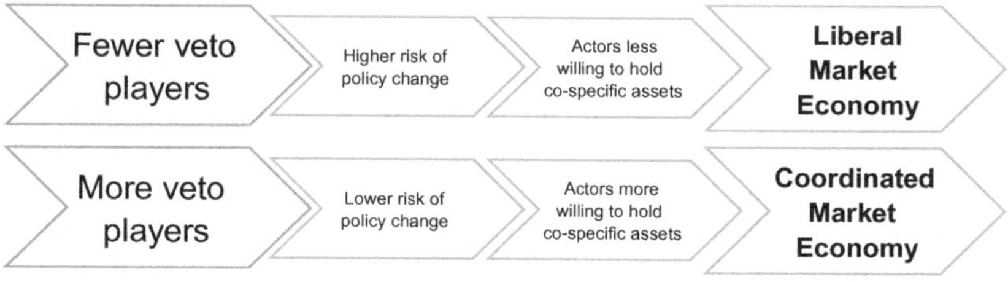

Fig. 1.1 Varieties of capitalism and the impact of veto players

This argument hinges on the perceptions and preferences of investors, managers, and workers (Gourevitch and Shinn 2005). Coordinative institutions reduce transaction costs but increase exposure to the risk of radical policy shifts. If radical policy shifts happen frequently, investors, workers, and managers will be hesitant to hold the co-specific assets that make up coordinated institutions because of the risks involved. Rather, they are more likely to maximize asset switchability, perceiving that transaction costs and the risk of managerial shirking are less of a liability than the risk of radical policy change. I will go into more detail on this below. Policy volatility is thus the key mechanism of the VoC argument linking veto players and types of capitalism (Hall and Soskice 2001; Gourevitch 2003; Gourevitch and Hawes 2002; Gourevitch and Shinn 2005).

Why would policy-makers engage in such radical policy reversals? If there is a change in government, the new government may wish to pursue a completely different policy agenda than the previous one. Thus, in countries where a small change in the vote may bring a new government into office, the anticipation of radical policy shifts makes co-specific investments too risky. In countries with coalition governments, where there are more veto players, such changes are less likely, thus encouraging co-specific investments and strong coordinative institutions. Initial efforts to test this framework in developed countries have met with some success (Gourevitch 2003; Gourevitch and Hawes 2002; Porta et al. 1999). But what of a country with a single veto player where there is little to no expectation of a change in government, such as in countries dominated by a single political party?

Single, Non-Alternating Veto Player Governments: Tsebelis' treatment of veto players suggests that in such a case, without alternation of the veto player, there would be low risk of radical policy shifts because that player would have already achieved her preferred policy (Tsebelis 1995). The result, according to the logic of the VoC framework, would be a coordinated system. The strong coordinating capabilities, such as apparent in newly industrialized countries (NICs) seem to support this expectation. On the other hand, both Cox and McCubbins and MacIntyre note that single veto player governments may have commitment problems and be generally irresolute (MacIntyre 2003a, b; Cox and McCubbins 2001). That is because, though the single veto player has had the opportunity to achieve her ideal policy positions, there are some issue areas where a policy-maker has incentive to move policy in one direction for a period of time and shift it radically later. Governsments with more veto players will have less trouble with this time-inconsistency problem than single veto player governments, suggesting that risk of radical policy shifts may remain higher in non-alternating single veto player governments than would be suggested by only looking at the implications of Tsebelis' argument. If this were so, we would expect single veto player autocracies to be liberal market economies.

Yet, in reality, liberal governance institutions remain weak in autocracies and there are many examples where an autocratic regime leads to an economy based on access to political rents that resembles neither the liberal nor the coordinated type characterized by the VoC framework. Though Hall and Soskice posit a third, Mediterranean model, it is not developed in depth and is wholly separate from the veto player argument (Hall and Soskice 2001, 21). Thus, these countries are unaccounted for in the two-ideal type VoC/VP framework and we are left with a puzzle: why do some single veto player regimes resemble coordinated market economies and others defy characterization in the VoC/VP framework? I describe a theory that in part explains this puzzle in the next chapter, but first I consider the opposite end of the veto player spectrum: governments with excessive veto players (EVP).

Excessive Veto Player Governments: As mentioned above, additional veto players are expected to result in coordinated governance institutions. Yet Italy, a country with a history of large coalition governments and hence a very high number of veto players, not only fails to resemble the coordinated ideal type, but defies categorization in the framework entirely. Why might countries with a very high number of veto players not act as expected? The VoC literature suggests that additional veto players will lead to the strengthening of coordinating institutions by constraining the ability of the government to radically change policies. Without the concern that policies affecting the industry in which they are engaged might change with little warning, owners, managers, and workers face less risk in investing in co-specific assets.

In contrast, Cox and McCubbins argue that once there are so many veto players that gridlock is reached, additional players will lead to policy balkanization (Cox and McCubbins 2001). This is when individual veto players capture specific agencies and ministries and pursue independent policies, in effect losing veto power over one another. The result is that "policy-making gets parsed out to numerous, relatively small, self-interested actors. Instead of a coherent majority making policy for the good of the nation—or at least for the good of the majority—this kind of atomistic policy-making is thought to lead to fragmented, incoherent policy that usurps the majority will and transforms it into specialized benefits for multiple minorities" (Cox and McCubbins 2001, 53). How does such a narrowly targeted policy environment impact the governance systems that develop? I will argue in the next chapter that it leads to a third, hierarchical variety of capitalism—where the pursuit of political access undermines both radical and incremental innovations.

The VoC argument offers a promising framework for explaining variation in the types of governance institutions that appear in developing countries. It argues that additional veto players increase the likelihood of having a coordinated, rather than liberal economic system. Three problems are apparent, however. First, it gives no explicit indication of what non-alternating single veto player regimes should look like. Even if we extrapolate from the source veto player material, we are unable to account for the types of governance systems we observe in many autocracies. Expanding the theoretical framework to account for autocracies allows for the inclusion of more observations where the underlying mechanism, micro-incentives created by the policy environment, are still at work. Second, Cox and McCubbins suggest that in cases with a particularly large number of veto players, policy will be narrowly targeted. It is unclear how this would affect the development of economic governance institutions. Third, there are many countries that defy easy classification into the liberal/coordinated dichotomy. The next chapter lays out a model that helps to resolve these issues.

Notes

1. Based on calculations from UN Comtrade.
2. The following two paragraphs are largely based upon Hall and Soskice (Hall and Soskice 2001).
3. It should be noted that in contrast with Hall and Soskice (2001), who treat Japan as a CME, Schneider (2013) describes Japan and Korea as a Network variant of capitalism. While the distinctions between Network and Coordinated systems are real and important, I have elected to use the characterization offered by Hall and Soskice for the following reasons. First, both rely on non-market relations in order to coordinate operations and reduce transaction costs. Though the network variants have different means of achieving this, the function they serve is similar. Thus, I prefer to view the Network Market Economy as a variant of CME. Second, the deductive framework developed here (see the next chapter) leads to no

clear expectation of when a country would develop network as opposed to coordinative systems—just that they would develop institutions that rely on non-market relationships and co-specific assets to reduce transaction costs. Should the framework developed in this book prove useful, a subsequent analysis of the determinants of the type of non-market arrangements utilized in different CMEs.

4. For more on veto players, see (Tsebelis 1995, 1999, 2002). For more on testing the relationship, see (Hall and Soskice 2001; Gourevitch 2003; Gourevitch and Hawes 2002; Gourevitch and Shinn 2005).

References

Cox, G. W., & McCubbins, M. (2001). The institutional determinants of economic policy outcomes. In S. Haggard & M. McCubbins (Eds.), *Presidents, parliaments, and policy* (pp. 21–63). Cambridge: Cambridge University Press.

Hall, P., & Soskice, D. (2001). *Varieties of capitalism: The institutional foundations of comparative advantage*. Oxford: Oxford University Press.

Gourevitch, P. (2003). Political determinants of corporate governance: Political context corporate impact. *Yale Law Journal, 112*(7), 1829–1881.

Gourevitch, P., & Hawes, M. (2002). The politics of choice among national production systems. *L'Année de La Régulation, 6*, 241–270.

Gourevitch, P., & Shinn, J. (2005). *Political power and corporate control: The new global politics of corporate governance*. Princeton, NJ: Princeton University Press.

MacIntyre, A. (2003a). Institutions and investors: The politics of the economic crisis in Southeast Asia. *International Organization, 55*(1), 81–122.

MacIntyre, A. (2003b). *The power of institutions: Political architecture and governance*. Ithaca, NY: Cornell University Press.

Porta, L., Lopez-de-Silanes, F., & Shleifer, A. (1999). Corporate ownership around the world. *Journal of Finance, 54*(2), 471–517.

Schneider, B. R. (2013). *Hierarchical capitalism in Latin America*. Cambridge: Cambridge University Press.

Tsebelis, G. (1995). Decision making in political systems: Veto players in presidentialism, parliamentarism, multicameralism and multipartyism. *British Journal of Political Science, 25*(3), 289–325.

Tsebelis, G. (1999). Veto players and law production in parliamentary democracies: An empirical analysis. *The American Political Science Review, 93*(3), 591–608.

Tsebelis, G. (2002). *Veto players: How political institutions work*. Princeton, NJ: Princeton University Press.

CHAPTER 2

Constraints and Development

In this book, I attempt to expand the VoC approach to include a wider set of countries. As laid out in the first chapter, there are important limitations in the applicability of the existing VoC/VP framework for explaining the variation of economic governance institutions in developing countries. This chapter develops an alternative framework for explaining these determinants by exploring the scholarly work on development.

The developmental state literature looks at the ability of governments to achieve rapid growth by intervening in the economy to overcome market failures in the provision of infrastructure and investment by promoting business directly, by picking winners, and by facilitating coordination among businesses (Gerschenkron 1962; Johnson 1982; Evans 1995; Noble 1998). Though the firm is given more of a prominent position in the VoC literature, it is also critical to the processes identified in the development literature. Government programs must be designed and implemented with industry input and buy-in. Businesses must choose to interact with each other and with the state in order for development programs and institutions to work; business interests must become embedded in development bureaucracies without capturing them (Evans 1995; Noble 1998).

Similarly, in coordinated market economies, economic actors must be willing to form long-term relations with each other, with suppliers, and with state institutions. They must be willing to share critical information about their activities and not sacrifice long-term growth opportunities

J.D. Moore, *Varieties of Capitalism in Southeast Asia*, The Political Economy of East Asia, DOI 10.1007/978-3-319-53700-9_2

for short-term profits. In other words, they must be willing to hold co-specific assets. As described above, these are risky to have in environments where policy change is common. The state can subsidize many of these endeavors, but the success of any such policy still depends on its credibility with business.

What factors will encourage the participation of business and the ultimate success of the developmental state? Autonomy of the bureaucracy from political forces is heavily cited (Evans 1995; Johnson 1982; Noble 1998). That is, if economic policy is designed by insulated technocrats to serve broad, rather than narrow, interests then actors will be willing to hold co-specific assets. If, however, policy-makers are captured and policy is designed to serve particularistic interests, a system of governance develops that is neither wholly coordinated nor wholly liberal. In this type of economic system, the availability of narrowly targeted policies provides owners, managers, and workers with incentives that dissuade them from holding co-specific assets. For example, firms that can access policy-makers for directly targeted benefits will be less willing to share information about their activities, plans, and capabilities with competitors, suppliers, and customers in order to achieve policy changes that benefit the industry as a whole. This is because the pathways of access themselves become important secrets that firms have extra incentive to keep secret. This sort of governance system has institutions which resemble Ben Schneider's hierarchical economic governance institutions (Schneider 2013).

The hierarchical market economy features governance institutions that revolve around personal and familial networks of loyalty and patronage. The extent of cooperation is limited to non-peak, family-based conglomerations of firms. This sort of hierarchical system may better characterize some of those cases that fall outside of the VoC categories. Thus, political systems that result in particularistic policy outcomes ought to have hierarchical economic governance institutions.

But in some respects, the autonomy of the bureaucracy is a placeholder for other variables. If the bureaucracy exists at the whim of the government, then whether or not it is autonomous depends on the willingness of the government to keep it so. The question becomes: when will states have the political will to keep the bureaucracy insulated while engaging business?

Some scholars focus on structural factors to explain variation in the political will of the state. Exposure to external military threats, breadth of political coalitions, and access to natural resources are expected to impact the ability of the state to insulate policy from narrow interests (Cummings 1998; Ross 1999; Waldner 1999). Doner, Ritchie, and Slater integrate these arguments into a single theory (Doner et al. 2005). They argue that some developing countries are better able to create "developmental institutions" because systemic vulnerabilities force them to. A combination of external threat, sensitivity to popular pressures, and resource scarcity will force a government to vigorously pursue upgrading so that it can afford the high levels of military spending and side payments required to stay in power. While the authors never explicitly refer to policy stability (other than macroeconomic) as a mechanism of this process, I submit that these vulnerable leaders will avoid policy volatility as it reduces credibility and increases uncertainty. Additionally, though the authors focus primarily on the impact of these variables at the time of state formation and consider them as nominal variables, I believe that the logic should apply as a matter of degree and throughout the lifespan of a country. It is unclear if it would have the same impact on democracies or countries with more than a single veto player. Both the Doner et al. article and Hicken and Ritchie's examination of Singapore suggest that it is at least applicable to single veto player contexts (Hicken and Ritchie 2002; Doner et al. 2005).

In addition to giving broadly targeted side payments, single veto player autocracies facing vulnerabilities are more motivated to find institutional mechanisms to overcome the time-inconsistency problem. This argument need not be entirely functionalist; it may be that, though motivated, an autocrat is unable to find the mix of institutions needed to signal policy stability. If so, however, the failure to subsequently provide sufficient resources to maintain broadside payments and military spending means that the regime will not last long. Also, I am not claiming that all authoritarian regimes are necessarily single veto player governments. Rather, the above discussion of autocracies refers to non-democracies controlled by single veto player governments.

Such institutional mechanisms may be deep business consultations or any interest representation short of outright veto power. Hicken and Ritchie and Doner, Hicken, and Ritchie have explored the viability of such non-veto consultative mechanisms in greater detail. For our purpose, it is enough to say that systemic vulnerability will motivate autocrats to overcome the time-consistency problem and commit to policy stability.[1]

2.1 Synthesis: Veto Players, Corruption, and Coordination

One strand of the VoC literature argues that the number of veto players will determine whether an economy resembles the liberal or coordinated ideal type. As noted above, a group of countries (including those with EVPs) emerges which does not fit into either of its main categories and the framework offers conflicting explanations as to why some single veto player autocracies resemble coordinated economies while others do not. The developmental state literature identifies an alternative economic system based on political rent seeking and provides a theory as to why some single veto player autocracies resemble coordinated economies while others do not. The presence or absence of systemic vulnerabilities will determine in part whether the policy environment is broadly targeted and stable, encouraging coordinative economic governance institutions or collusive, encouraging hierarchical governance institutions.

Adding a third, hierarchical market economy (HME) to the two present in the VoC framework can greatly improve its utility in explaining governance systems in developing countries. Does not this cause major damage to the parsimony of the veto-player model? There is some debate on this tradeoff in the larger comparative capitalisms literature. Colin Crouch criticizes the VoC framework for missing important complexities because of its parsimony (Crouch 2005a, b). Future work, he argues, should include more types and identify the strength of institutions from each type in a given governance system. While adding a third type is far shy of the complexity that Crouch is advocating, I argue that retaining the integrity of the veto player framework, with its clear deductively derived expectations, is worth the potential loss of descriptive accuracy. On the other hand, I agree with and employ Crouch's "analytical" approach to evaluating types of institutions. This approach identifies the strength of each of the potential types of governance institutions rather than simply characterizing an economy as one, single type. In addition to achieving greater accuracy, this will enable us to observe changes over time (Crouch 2005a).

What exactly would the institutions in a hierarchical governance system look like? The competition for access to policy-makers becomes the key force in hierarchical governance systems. The potential for rents provides incentives for economic actors to create and make use of institutional structures that maximize access. Patron–client ties are a defining feature of such systems. It is worth noting here that patron–client ties are typically informal institutional relationships. That is, they are not maintained via legal contracts or specified in organizational charts. To be sure, the relationships may be glimpsed now and again in the formal institutional arrangement, for example in the makeup of a firm's boards of directors, but the substance of the relationships pre-exists these formal ties and does not substantively rely upon them.[2]

In the realm of corporate governance, the availability of rents means a substantially different set of incentives facing investors. Just as with liberal systems, investors in a hierarchical system are very concerned by risks. If a competitor suddenly gains access to officials or the actor finds himself out of favor with the government, his access to rents may suffer. As such, investors will be unwilling to concentrate their holdings in a single industry. On the other hand, they are unwilling to rely on diffuse shareholding to allay these risks because the background legal institutions provide little protection from managerial shirking or expropriation by controlling shareholders. Rather, investors must make use of other institutions which do not rely on the state to limit exposure. Often this means a reliance on patron–client or ethnic/communal ties. Investors can then spread their assets over many industries through bonds of power or trust rather than bonds of law. Such conglomerations also have the benefit of enhancing the investor's political clout and access to subsequent rents, providing firms with a competitive edge based on access rather than either incremental or radical innovations. This is in agreement with Schneider's characterization of hierarchical corporate governance in Latin America (Schneider 2013).

Of course, conglomerated business groups can also be efficient more generally when there are many benefits from economies of scope. Particularly in developing countries, where managerial and technological knowledge-based assets are in short supply, there may be great benefits for a particular firm to utilize its accumulated knowledge-based assets in more than one product category. Indeed, the Japanese Keiretsu and Korean Chaebol had success in using diversified business groups to exploit economies of scope at earlier stages of developments (Amsden 2001; Feenstra and Hamilton 2006). While there is no reason to think that diversified family conglomerates in hierarchical market economies would not want to economize in a similar fashion, the expectation is that the extent of diversification in hierarchical market economies will be substantially wider than can be attributed to economies of scope.

That is, while there may be many knowledge-based assets acquired in the process of manufacturing textiles that are applicable to the manufacturing of shoes, it is unlikely that there will be many that are applicable to real-estate.

Inter-firm ties in a hierarchical system will be more developed than in a liberal system but weaker than in a coordinated system. The weakness of the legal system limits the willingness of firms to share sensitive information with competitors. Supply lines may be run internally in large conglomerates. While this may reduce the chances for fraud, there is no guarantee that the goods will be of adequate quality or cost. Additionally, because the owners are not heavily concentrated in the relevant industry, there will be less benefit from accumulated, specialized knowledge.

The complementarities inherent in hierarchical market economies (HME) are self-reinforcing as in the ideal-type CMEs and LMEs, but they are not positive in the same way. Each hierarchical governance institution in an economy does not increase the returns to other hierarchical EGIs so much as reduce the returns to other non-hierarchical Economic Governance Institutions (EGI). The absence of worker training institutions for either general or specific skills will lead to an unskilled workforce. With such a workforce, foreign MNCs are unlikely to invest in any production activities that require skilled workers. Without any job opportunities for skilled labor, workers are unwilling to invest in skills. The same holds true for domestic firms (Schneider 2013).

Firms and conglomerates built around individual families with political access are likely to want to limit the flow of information about current and future firm activities to protect their political rents. Thus, they are unlikely to hire, promote, or train workers to critical managerial or engineering positions without direct familial or patron–client ties. This both significantly limits the demand for skilled labor in the market and dulls the innovative (both incremental and radical) capacities of the firm. Similar problems will occur in attempts to form strong inter-firm governance institutions. Firms will be even more hesitant to share information about operations with competitors as such information may reveal patterns of access that could lead to exposure. With operations spread around several industries, family conglomerates would also be hesitant to become too involved in any one (Schneider 2013).

A particularistic policy environment will result in a hierarchical governance system because access to policy-makers becomes the most effective way for firms and investors to maximize profits and minimize risks. The returns to investments in attaining political access become higher than the returns to investments in either incremental or radical innovations. Because medium-term firm strategies are made conditional on the opportunities created by policy-makers and because firms will want to prevent evidence of such collusive relationships from being made public, they will limit the involvement of employees in the formulation of these plans. Without active engagement of skilled, senior employees, neither incremental nor radical innovation becomes possible for such access-centered firms.

Three categories result: liberal, coordinated, and hierarchical governance systems. As with the VoC argument, veto players act as constraints. For single veto player governments without alternation, we would expect the lack of constraints on rent-seeking to lead to a particularistic policy environment and a hierarchical system unless systemic vulnerabilities serve as an alternative form of constraint. Thus, systemic vulnerability conditions the impact of the single veto player. Additional players add additional constraints on the government's ability to radically change policies or provide narrowly targeted rents. At the high extreme, however, balkanization and/or logrolling occurs so that narrowly targeted rents are pervasive throughout the economy and hierarchical institutions develop. Figure 2.1 provides a graphical representation of the argument (which represents extreme high and low exceptions to the linear relationship presented in Fig. 1.1).

Though the model developed here is designed to account for the full spectrum of governance systems, I focus the remainder of this book on developing and testing the implications of the most novel elements of this framework: the single veto player autocracies and the countries with EVP governments.

2.2 Cases and Concepts

This book evaluates the explanatory power of my typological framework in accounting for the evolution of economic governance institutions in Thailand, Malaysia, and Singapore. These countries were selected because they feature within-case variation on the key variables of this study. In looking intensively at a smaller number of cases, I can determine in part whether the degree of vulnerability and the number of veto players had the expected impact and whether the mechanisms

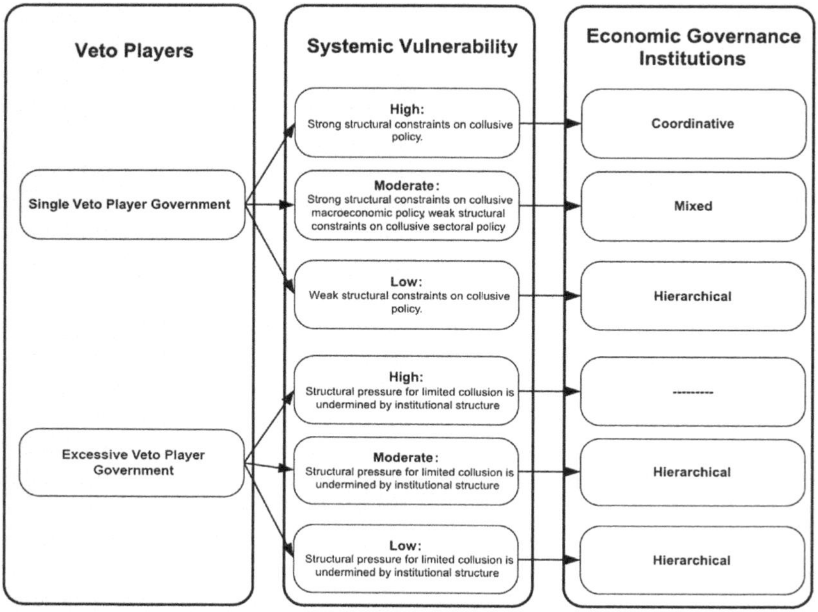

Fig. 2.1 Typological framework

hypothesized by the theory are connecting cause to effect. The variation observed in Thailand is longitudinal. Here I am able to control for much, noting how changes in the number of veto players and the degree of vulnerability result in changes in the policy environment and ultimately governance institutions. In Malaysia, by contrast, the variation is regional. Much is held common because of the same national context, but historically contingent regional differences have resulted in variation in the degree of vulnerability—which leads us to expect divergent outcomes. Although Singapore only offers a single observation for the purposes of this study, it is especially valuable for comparing the outcomes across each of the countries.

In Thailand, changes in national political institutions and the larger political environment make for six distinct periods, with both single veto player and excessive veto player governments facing low to high levels of vulnerability. In Chap. 3, I explore the impact of these changing circumstances on the policy environment and on patterns of economic

Table 2.1 Case selection

	Systemic vulnerability		
	Low	*Moderate*	*High*
One veto player	Post 1969 (MY); Single party (TH); Military rule (TH)	Semi-democracy (TH),[a] Pre 1969 (MY)	Singapore, Penang (MY)
Excessive veto players	Coalitional democracy (TH)	Post-crisis (TH)	Instability period (TH)[b]

[a]In this period there was a single veto player in charge of macro policies and an EVP coalition in charge of sectoral/micro policies

[b]I do not have a case that fits in this cell of the typology but the theoretical argument suggests that such a case could not exist long (i.e. it would be overthrown, invaded, or reformed with fewer veto players). I will briefly discuss the instability period in Thailand to explain how and why an EVP government ought not to be possible in a high vulnerability environment

governance. This also allows me to observe the process of institutional change. In Malaysia, a combination of factors caused the Penang state government to be in a much more vulnerable position than the rest of the country. As such, I compare the types of economic governance institutions that developed in each in Chap. 4. In Chap. 5, I evaluate the evolution of the policy environment and economic governance in Singapore, where a single veto player government faced high vulnerability. In Chap. 6, I make comparisons across the cases and assess the framework as a whole. The countries selected are, of course, quite diverse. These cases allow me to end up with some modest, contingent generalizations about the larger population of the single and EVP sub types. The table situates the observations within the framework (Table 2.1).

These cases also allow for the elimination of potential rival explanations. Some observers have suggested that cultural traits may account for unique Asian types of capitalism. In particular, a Sino variant of capitalism has received attention in the popular and academic analyses of Asian capitalism. It is thought to produce unique characteristics, influenced by social and religious cultural attributes (Gomez and Xiao 2004; Tanzer 1994; Weidenbaum and Hughes 1996). I compare three economies dominated by ethnically Chinese actors: Singapore, Malaysia, and Thailand which should produce quite distinct governance systems according to the theoretical framework. If, however, the power of culture is determinative, those countries should produce similar outcomes.

Alternatively, it may be that ethnic divisions in general, rather than the attributes of any specific culture, prevent the type of economy-wide collaboration necessary for coordinated governance (Banerjee et al. 2005; Alesina et al. 1999; Miguel and Gugerty 2005). Singapore and Malaysia feature ethnic heterogeneity. If ethnic homogeneity or inter-ethnic harmony is necessary for coordination, we would expect the absence of coordinative institutions, despite what is predicted by the framework. Because I am observing changes over time, I will also be able to evaluate the effects of alternation in the identity of veto players.

Another possible alternative argument is that growing US influence, increasing capital mobility, and the intellectual hegemony of neoliberal principles are leading to a global growth of LME institutions. This perspective, which parallels the institutional convergence critique of the Varieties of Capitalism perspective, should lead to an outcome whereby countries' institutions increasingly morph into liberal governance systems to comply with the interests of short-term investors (Hall and Thelen 2009; Howell 2017). Because I am evaluating the strength of each type of governance system, I will be able to observe the relative changes in the strength of liberal institutions.

Another possibility is that multinational corporations engaging in foreign direct investments or forming joint ventures will simply transplant or recreate their home country governance institutions (Yeung and Coe 2015, 49). A more nuanced version of this argument, derived from the global value chain (GVC) approach, would be that lead firms may relocate segments of their value chain to specific countries depending on the innovative and coordinative capacities in those countries (Yeung and Coe 2015; Coe and Yeung 2015; Barrientos et al. 2011; Lane and Probert 2009). For example, a lead firm may want product design and high value-added manufacturing to take place in a country with strong coordinative institutions while they relegate simple assembly and more mature manufacturing to occur in places with hierarchical institutions because of the associated pool of low-cost, low-skilled labor.

It is possible that systemic vulnerability has an indirect effect on the type of governance system by influencing the number of veto players in addition to the direct influence it has on the governance system. This may result in a causally complex, intervening, causally shallow or even spurious relationship between the number of veto players and the type of governance system (George and Bennett 2005). Further research must be done to explore the effects of vulnerability on the number of veto players in government. As noted earlier, I have limited this book to the study of subtypes of the larger veto player framework. I thus limit my conclusions to contingent generalizations regarding the single and EVP subtypes (albeit with highly suggestive implications for the larger VoC framework). For single veto player governments, the framework predicts systemic vulnerability to be determinative. For EVP governments it predicts systemic vulnerability to have no effect. Whether or not the systemic vulnerability had a prior effect on the number of veto players should not bias my results since I am not making explicit generalizations about the other possible subtypes. If the results of this analysis suggest that further testing of this modified framework as a whole is warranted, the potential indirect effect of systemic vulnerability by means of affecting the number of veto players must be tested as well (i.e. endogeneity). To further this end, this project includes a preliminary investigation into this question.

Looking at the difference between MNC behavior in Penang and the rest of Malaysia is especially informative here. If MNCs set up similar operations in both areas but strong coordinative institutions develop in one but not the other, then the MNC argument is not a sufficient explanation. Additionally, in both Penang and Singapore, the timing of the creation of the institutions vis-à-vis the arrival of MNCs will be relevant. The framework employed here suggests that the policy environment and the resultant governance institutions will condition MNC strategies. That is, if there is a stable, broadly targeted policy environment, MNCs will employ strategies that make use of the reduced transaction costs embodied in CME institutions, but if there is a particularist policy environment, MNCs will use hierarchical structures to mitigate risks. Thus, the MNC deterministic approach and my approach offer conflicting expectations.

The second alternative, the undeveloped argument is that strong consultative mechanisms, whereby economic actors have (non-veto) participation in policy-making, may make policy changes predictable to these actors (Hicken and Ritchie 2002; Doner et al. 2009). If this is the case, these actors may be willing to form co-specific assets despite the potential for policy changes in single veto player regimes, because they will occur for predictable reasons. Here, tracing policy changes in Singapore and Penang and evaluating changes in risk perceptions and willingness to form co-specific assets of actors will be useful in evaluating this possibility. I label these as undeveloped arguments rather than as alternative theories because it is not clear what types of MNCs would prefer strong coordinating institutions or what types of consultations with economic actors are a sufficient signal to make policy changes predictable.

I am attempting to explain the variance of economic governance institutions in the electronics and electrical appliance industries. I have selected this sector for several reasons. Successful electronics production generally is technically demanding and typically represents entry into a higher value-added segment of the global economy. Despite this, however, there is ample room for producers to specialize in simple assembly and lower value segments of this global value chain. Electrical appliance and electronics production, in particular, contains a range of technologies that may be possible for producers to mimic—but which would require stronger cooperative capacities to absorb, thus creating strong incentives to form cooperative institutions where the political environment permits (Lall 1998).

Another advantage of using the electronics and electrical appliance industries is that they have emerged as important sectors for each of the Southeast Asian countries selected in this study. In the last 50 years, Thailand has become a major exporter in some mature appliance subsectors such as air conditioning and refrigerator manufacturing. All three countries have been generally successful in exporting within the computer component industry, with important variation in the degree to which local firms have upgraded from simple assembly to higher value segments of the global electronics value chain. Other research has been done looking at the importance of developmental state institutions and national innovation systems in explaining the various levels of success in upgrading in this industry (Intarakumnerd et al. 2002; McKendrick et al. 2000). This book will contribute to this literature by offering a political explanation that accounts for both of these more proximate explanations.

For each of the periods and regions studied, I describe the overall, economy-wide economic governance institutions and then proceed to go into detail on governance in the electronics and electrical industries.

Institutions tend to be especially abstract and vaguely understood, even by the actors that regularly interact with them. Though I am investigating economic governance institutions using a framework that has been employed elsewhere, previous analyses offer limited guidance. This is because previous studies have differed in their conceptualization of economic governance institutions, have often preferred to use already available proxy indicators, and because I am substantially expanding the diversity of cases to which the framework is applied.

Hall and Soskice have differentiated between two ideal types of governance systems: liberal and coordinated (Hall and Soskice 2001). Because they were primarily concerned with broadly characterizing the ideal types and their innovational outcomes, they did not provide precise indicators. By evaluating "degrees of coordination" in corporate governance institutions, Gourevitch and Shinn offer clearer indicators and a more ordinal measure, along the lines recommended by Crouch (Gourevitch and Shinn 2005). But because they still base their analysis on a dichotomous typology, they mischaracterize observations that have stronger coordinating institutions than exist in liberal systems but that operate with a different internal logic than coordinated institutions.

Though the VoC scholars have identified five such institutions, I am focusing on two: inter-firm linkage and corporate governance institutions. I also evaluate recent research by Ritchie concerning a third, worker training institutions (Ritchie 2010). Corporate governance institutions structure the relationship between investors and firms. They are central to much of the work on this literature and have a powerful impact on the structure of the economy as a whole (Gourevitch and Hawes 2002; Gourevitch and Shinn 2005; Gourevitch 2003). Inter-firm linkage institutions structure the relationships among firms, both horizontally and vertically. Linkages and linkage institutions such as business associations are often cited as important by the development literature (Brimble and Doner 2007).

I focus my attention on those institutions for which data are available. This necessarily means that institutions that were considered or attempted but were unsuccessful are not observed. If this leads to any bias, it will be that I view institutions as weaker than they may be in actuality. Though I make every effort to limit exposure to this by gathering as much information as possible, I acknowledge this potential for bias. There may be an additional problem for informal institutions generally and collusive informal institutions in particular. The longitudinal approach of this book allows us to overcome this problem to some degree by comparing the changing manifestations of these informal institutions over time. I have no expectation that the actors would have greater or lesser ability to hide such informal institutions in one period than another.

Much of this analysis will be based on evaluating changes in formal and informal economic governance institutions that emerge in response to changes in the overall policy environment. As Hall and Thelen note, this must be done with care as informal practices may remain despite formal institutional changes and informal practices may shift despite no obvious change in the formal institutions (Hall and Thelen 2009; Thelen 2004). Thus, I look for evidence of these changing practices in addition to changing institutions.

Corporate governance institutions structure the relationship between investors and firms. Coordinative corporate governance institutions rely on either patient, concentrated bank credit that allows lending which stimulates long-term growth rather than quick returns or networks of cross-shareholding firms that have a real stake in each other's operations (Figs. 2.2 and 2.3).

The primary indicator for the strength of liberal corporate governance institutions is the proportion of publicly listed firms that are widely held. I rely on the classification system of Porta et al. for this assessment (Porta et al. 1999). If companies do not use stock markets to raise external funds, I consider liberal corporate governance institutions weak. Likewise, the strength of coordinated corporate governance institutions is assessed by looking at the proportion of publicly listed firms that rely on widely held financial institutions. Of course, the Japanese "network" version of coordinated corporate governance relies on patterns of cross-shareholding more than bank-lending. So, I evaluate whether there is a high degree of non-pyramid, cross-shareholding in listed firms.

In HMEs, firms access funding using resources spread throughout family-dominated business conglomerations. External funding coming from outside of these familial channels are limited because of the high risk of the expropriation of firm value by controlling shareholders. This same concern also prevents the development of widely-held financial institutions (Fig. 2.4).

It is important to note that the formal distinctions listed above can be misleading. Firms listed in capital markets can be hierarchically controlled through pyramid shareholding arrangements and financial institutions may not be widely held and use access potential, rather than growth potential to assess long-term profitability. Thus, where possible, I take the degree of pyramid shareholding structures and family dominance of financial institutions into account when deciding whether a particular group's finances are hierarchically structured.

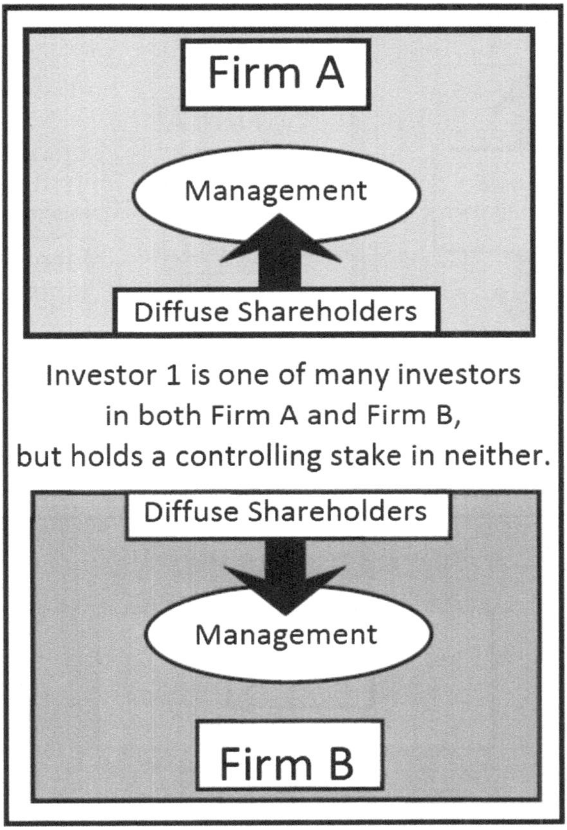

Fig. 2.2 Firm structure under liberal corporate governance systems

Inter-firm linkage institutions (ILI) structure the relationships between companies, both horizontally and vertically. Evaluating ILIs is not quite as clear-cut as evaluating corporate governance institutions. There are no ready-made, easily quantifiable indicators that can show conclusively when coordinated, liberal, or hierarchical inter-firm institutions are dominant in an economy. The main way of distinguishing between types of ILIs is by characterizing the nature of activities they undertake. In liberal systems, firms use market signals to determine the

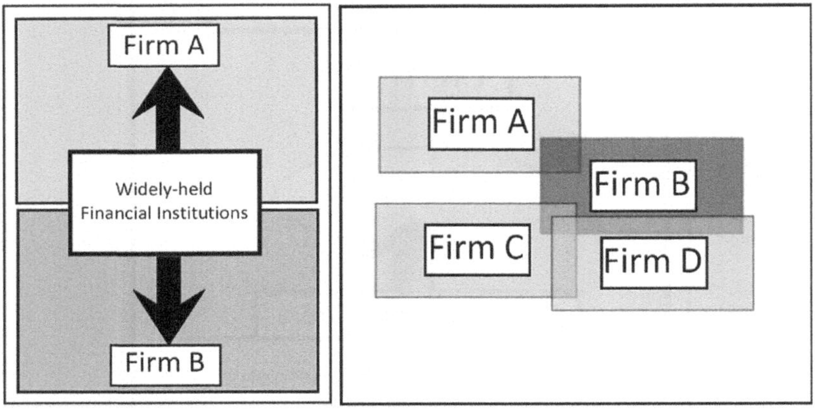

Fig. 2.3 Firm structure under coordinated corporate governance systems

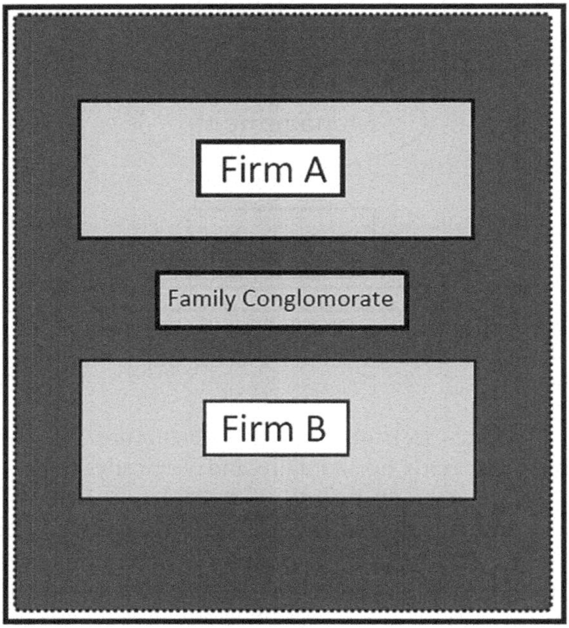

Fig. 2.4 Firm structure under hierarchical corporate governance systems

price and quantity of goods to exchange with suppliers and customers and activities beyond arms-length contracting are largely foregone. In coordinated systems, firms use long-term relationships with suppliers and customers that are much less dependent on current market signals and engage in a wide variety of cooperative activities. In a hierarchical system, firms also rely on non-market relationships but use other sources of power to facilitate limited, typically oligopolistic linkages.

Thus, it is quite likely that ILIs with similar sounding names may be performing quite different operations in the different systems. An apparel manufacturers association may, for example, engage in limited lobbying for tariff reform in a liberal system, in a wide range of activities including joint research, training, and government consultation in a coordinated system, and in cartel pricing in a hierarchical system.

For each observation, I characterize the nature of linkage activities engaged in by the main inter-firm organizations. Linkage institutions that are predominantly engaged in arms-length, market-based activities with little or no coordinative activities are considered liberal. Linkage institutions that are engaging in activities requiring substantial coordinative capacities are considered coordinative. Linkage institutions are serving the interests of the most powerful firms are treated as hierarchical. Very large firms may sometimes find it in their interest to engage in activities with positive externalities that will benefit the entire sector. These activities may include creating horizontal and vertical organizations that serve the interests of the sector. Although such behavior is initiated by large firms for self-interested reasons, I count it as evidence of coordinative inter-firm institutions when the actions of the resulting institutions serve the interests of the horizontal or vertical bodies broadly.

According to the framework employed here, veto players and levels of systemic vulnerability are thought to jointly determine the nature of the above-identified economic governance institutions. Veto players are actors whose assent is required for change to the policy status quo to occur. I limit the scope of this project to single, non-alternating veto player regimes and countries with a very high number of veto players.[3] Following MacIntyre, I chose not to focus on ideology, but rather considered the number of discrete, partisan actors who have formal veto authority over the particular policy space (MacIntyre 2003a, b). Where factions are potentially important players within collective veto players, I use the level of direct, zero-sum competition among factions to determine whether to treat them as veto players. So, though military factions may be important actors within a junta, they are only counted as separate veto players where they are actively trying to undermine one another via promotion channels or a coup. Likewise, a faction within a political party will only be counted as a separate veto player if it competes for votes with other factions in the same party.

Though some have suggested that additional veto players may have nonlinear effects on a variety of outcomes, none have specified precisely where such a threshold would be (MacIntyre 2003b; Cox and McCubbins 2001). The observations I use to test the EVP portion of the framework represent cases at the extreme of existing veto player scales. If any observations should exhibit the qualities hypothesized, it should be these. Should the cases studied here behave as indicated by the framework, future quantitative tests may be able to pinpoint exactly where the deadlock-threshold may be.

I distinguish between macro- and microeconomic policy stability because, while both are important for actors' perceptions of the risks involved in forming coordinating institutions, they may be decided by different numbers of veto players. Additionally, they may be of unequal importance. It may be that the presence of particularistic interests in macro policy is more likely to result in highly hierarchical institutions than in micro policy.

Systemic vulnerability, which is expected to condition the impact of single veto player governments, is assessed along a three-value ordinal scale and has three critical elements: external threat, resource scarcity, and sensitivity to unrest. Rather than focus on these elements at the time of state formation as Doner, Ritchie, and Slater and Ritchie have done, I relax the assumption of path-dependency and assess changing values over time (Ritchie 2010; Doner et al. 2005).

Ritchie offers some proxy indicators for the level of external threat (Ritchie 2010). First, he uses a count of the number of conflicts a state is involved in, based on the Correlates of War Project (Small and Singer 2006). While this is a reasonable proxy indicator, it lacks precision on two critical fronts. First, it is unable to differentiate between conflicts where the survival of the regime in power is at risk and those where it is not. Second, it is unable to distinguish between cold wars and hot ones. He also uses military expenditures as a percentage of GDP. As military spending is an important causal mechanism in this framework, linking the level of external threat to the nature of the policy environment, I report it in that capacity as a measure of external threat. I follow Doner et al. in evaluating the degree to which overtly hostile countries have a credible potential to invade (Doner et al. 2005).

Following both Ritchie and Doner et al., I base my assessment of resource scarcity on the importance of natural resource extraction to an economy (Doner et al. 2005; Ritchie 2010). The value of commodity exports as a fraction of GDP—taken from Sachs and Warner (1997). To this, I add an assessment of aid inflows as a percentage of GDP, for these can likewise soften budget constraints.

Ritchie measures coalitional breadth using several alternative indicators (Ritchie 2010). First, he uses an index created by Bueno de Mesquita et al. to measure the size of the winning coalition in a country (Bueno de Mesquita et al. 2003). As Ritchie notes, this measure relies heavily on voting and elections, which are not necessary for a coalition to be considered broad in the systemic vulnerability model (Doner et al. 2005). Second, he looks at the degree of societal inequality. Again, this represents an important causal mechanism in my framework and is too related to the policy environment to be useful as an indicator of coalitional breadth/sensitivity to unrest. Following Doner et al., I focus specifically on the degree to which the government relies on the support or acquiescence of a majority of the population in order to maintain power (Doner et al. 2005).

Together, the number of veto players and the level of systemic vulnerability are expected to influence economic governance institutions by shaping the policy environment and thus the micro incentives facing workers, investors, and managers. As mentioned above, this framework distinguishes between macroeconomic policy and sectoral policy environments. In practice, the boundary lines between macro and sectoral policies may not be completely distinct. Macroeconomic policy areas, including fiscal, monetary, exchange rate, and trade policies, can be undermined or circumvented by sectoral policies such as tariff exemptions and export subsidies. For each type of policy environment, I evaluate the degree of policy volatility and the degree to which policies are narrowly targeted.

In the work that has posited a link between the number of veto players and the VoC, the degree to which economic actors fear radical shifts in economic policy has been of chief concern. But there is an important difference between a government changing policy in a consistent manner in response to an external event and a government changing policy in a haphazard manner for domestic political reasons. If, for example, an external shock occurs that would warrant some sort of stimulus according to orthodox macroeconomic theory, a mechanical evaluation of changes in policy on the ground may lead one to characterize as volatile, a policy environment in which investors might not actually fear radical policy change. Thus, in assessing the volatility of the policy environment, I try to be as clear and explicit as possible in indicating when a given policy change might be a predictable response to external circumstances and not evidence of volatility. I make this evaluation based on secondary analyses of the global economic circumstances of the time.

I argue that a particularistic policy environment incentivizes economic actors to engage in competition for political access that narrows the range of economic governance institutions they can establish. In a broad sense, particularistic economic policies are those that benefit specific groups at the expense of overall economic welfare. Unfortunately, not all economic policy changes involve Pareto-improvements. Even if a policy change improves the economy as a whole, there are usually some who lose out. Ideally, it would be easy to clearly differentiate between actors that seek compensation for policies that are harmful to them but led to net welfare improvements for the economy as a whole, and actors that seek to achieve their preferred policies regardless of their impact on the whole economy. For each category of economic policy, I specify the ways in which policy might be particularistic and the signs I look for in evaluating the degree of particularism.

Macroeconomic policy includes monetary, exchange rate, and fiscal policies. Monetary policy deals with the money supply and includes interest rates, reserve ratios, and the regulation of financial institutions. Exchange rate policy deals with the relative value of the currency and includes capital controls, foreign exchange reserves, and interventions in the foreign exchange market. Fiscal policy deals with the balance between state revenues and expenditures. For this macroeconomic component, I am focusing on changes in the overall amount of taxation and spending. I consider the macroeconomic policy environment predictable when governments consistently follow a clearly articulated policy objective (a balanced budget, counter-cyclical policy, or economic stimulus policy). Macroeconomic policy environment is unpredictable when a government or successive governments fail to do so. The policy environment is particularistic when there is a fiercely competitive battle to influence the size of the budget, interest rate level, or exchange rate level (since the battle to influence the distribution of the budget is considered in the sectoral policy environment).

Sectoral policy deals with government efforts to intervene in the market to achieve some particular set of goals. This can include attempts to achieve net-welfare enhancing goals such as limiting behaviors with negative externalities and promoting behaviors with positive externalities, but it can also include attempts to use government policies to assist particular well-connected firms at the expense of their competitors and consumers. The policies include regulatory policies, direct subsidies, credit guarantees, tax exemptions, and the provision of government contracts.

I consider the sectoral policy environment predictable when governments consistently follow a clearly articulated policy objective. The sectoral policy environment is unpredictable when a government or successive governments fail to do so and policy oscillates significantly over time. The policy environment is particularistic when sectoral policies are targeted at particular firms with very little clearly articulated economic rationale.

In Chaps. 3 through 5, I evaluate the impact of the number of veto players and the degree of vulnerability on the policy environment—and the impact of changes in the policy environment on the nature of corporate governance and inter-firm linkage institutions in Thailand, Malaysia, and Singapore. These utilize within-case comparisons, some longitudinal and some cross-sectional. In Chap. 6, I take a larger view and evaluate the ability of this typology to explain variation across these three countries.

Notes

1. See Hicken and Ritchie (2002); Doner et al. (2005) Of course, it may be that the government fails to do this or put strong developmental institutions in place. In such cases, it risks being replaced by invasion or mass uprising.
2. Not all such informal ties need be based on political rents, of course. The literature of capitalism in Asia points to informal bonds of trust, family, and shared ethnicity as leading to improvements in coordination and efficiency in Japan, South Korea, and Taiwan (Lincoln and Gerlach 1992; Feenstra and Hamilton 2006; Amsden 2001; Redding 1996).
3. Note here that I'm focused on the expectation of alternation of the veto player. The key is whether actors making the decision to participate in various types of governance institutions believe the government will remain in power.

References

Alesina, A., Baqir, R., & Easterly, W. (1999). Public goods and ethnic divisions. *Quarterly Journal of Economics, 114*(4), 1243–1284.

Amsden, A. H. (2001). *The rise of the rest, 1850–2000: Late industrialization outside the North Atlantic economies.* Oxford: Oxford University Press.

Banerjee, A., Iyer, L., & Somanathan, R. (2005). History, social divisions, and public goods in rural India. *Journal of the European Economic Association, 3*(2–3), 639–647.

Barrientos, S., Gereffi, G., & Rossi, A. (2011). Economic and social upgrading in global production networks. *International Labour Review, 150*(3), 319–340.

Brimble, P., & Doner, R. F. (2007). University-industry linkages and economic development: The case of Thailand. *World Development, 35*(6), 1021–1036.

Bueno de Mesquita, B., Smith, A., Siverson, R. M., & Morrow, J. D. (2003). *The logic of political survival.* Cambridge, MA: Massachusetts Institute of Technology.

Coe, N. M., & Yeung, H. W. (2015). *Global production networks: Theorizing economic development in an interconnected world.* Oxford: Oxford University Press.

Cox, G. W., & McCubbins, M. (2001). The institutional determinants of economic policy outcomes. In S. Haggard & M. McCubbins (Eds.), *Presidents, parliaments, and policy* (pp. 21–63). Cambridge: Cambridge University Press.

Crouch, C. (2005a). *Capitalist diversity and change: Recombinant governance and institutional entrepreneurs.* Oxford: Oxford University Press.

Crouch, C. (2005b). Models of capitalism. *New Political Economy, 10*(4), 439–456.

Cummings, M. W. (1998). National security and the rise of the developmental state in South Korean and Taiwan. In H. S. Rowen (Ed.), *Behind East Asian growth: The political and social foundations of prosperity.* London: Routledge.

Doner, R. F., Ritchie, B., & Slater, D. (2005). Systemic vulnerability and the origins of developmental states: Northeast and Southeast Asia in comparative perspective. *International Organization, 59*(2), 327–361.

Doner, R. F., Hicken, A., & Ritchie, B. (2009). Political challenges of innovation in the developing world. *Review of Policy Research, 26*(1–2), 151–171.

Evans, P. B. (1995). *Embedded autonomy: States and industrial transformation* (Vol. 2011). Princeton: Princeton University Press.

Feenstra, R. C., & Hamilton, G. G. (2006). *Emergent economies, divergent paths: Economic organization and international trade in South Korea and Taiwan.* Cambridge: Cambridge University Press. doi:10.1086/648632.

George, A. L., & Bennett, A. (2005). *Case studies and theory development in the social sciences.* Cambridge: The MIT Press.

Gerschenkron, A. (1962). *Economic backwardness in historical perspective.* Cambridge: Belknap Press of Harvard University Press.
Gomez, E. T., & Xiao, X. (2004). *Chinese enterprise, transnationalism, and identity.* London: Routledge.
Gourevitch, P., & Hawes, M. (2002). The politics of choice among national production systems. *L'Année de La Régulation, 6,* 241–270.
Gourevitch, P. (2003). Political determinants of corporate governance: Political context, corporate impact. *Yale Law Journal, 112*(7), 1829–1881.
Gourevitch, P., & Shinn, J. (2005). *Political power and corporate control: The new global politics of corporate governance.* Princeton: Princeton University Press.
Hall, P., & Soskice, D. (2001). *Varieties of capitalism: The institutional foundations of comparative advantage.* Oxford: Oxford University Press.
Hall, P., & Thelen, K. (2009). Institutional change in varieties of capitalism. *Socio-Economic Review, 7,* 7–34. doi:10.1093/ser/mwn020.
Hicken, A., & Ritchie, B. (2002). *The origin of credibility enhancing institutions in Southeast Asia. Paper delivered at the American Political Science annual meeting.*
Howell, C. (2017). Review: Varieties of capitalism: And then there was one? Reviewed work(s): Varieties of capitalism: The Institutional Foundations of Comparative Advantage by Peter Hall and David Soskice; The Origins of Nonliberal Capitalism: Germany and Japan in.
Intarakumnerd, P., Chairatana, P., & Tangchitpiboon, T. (2002). National innovation system in less successful developing countries: The case of Thailand. *Research Policy, 31*(8–9), 1445–1457.
Johnson, C. (1982). *MITI and the Japanese miracle: Growth of industrial policy: 1925–1975.* California: Stanford University Press.
Lall, S. (1998). Technology and human capital in maturing Asian countries. *Science Technology & Society, 3*(1), 11.
Lane, C., & Probert, J. (2009). *National capitalisms, global production networks: Fashioning the value chain in the UK, US, and Germany.* Oxford: Oxford University Press. http://doi.org/10.1093/acprof:oso/9780199214815.001.0001.
Lincoln, J. R., & Gerlach, M. L. (1992). *Japan's network economy. Social sciences.*
MacIntyre, A. (2003a). Institutions and investors: The politics of the economic crisis in Southeast Asia. *International Organization, 55*(1), 81–122.
MacIntyre, A. (2003b). *The power of institutions: Political architecture and governance.* Ithaca: Cornell University Press.
McKendrick, D., Doner, R. F., & Haggard, S. (2000). *From Silicon Valley to Singapore: Location and competitive advantage in the hard disk drive industry.* Stanford: Stanford University Press.
Miguel, E., & Gugerty, M. K. (2005). Ethnic diversity, social sanctions, and public goods in Kenya. *Journal of Public Economics, 89*(11–12), 2325–2368.
Noble, G. W. (1998). *Collective action in East Asia: How ruling parties shape industrial policy.* Ithaca: Cornell University Press.

Porta, L., Lopez-de-Silanes, F., & Shleifer, A. (1999). Corporate ownership around the world. *Journal of Finance, 54*(2), 471–517.
Redding, S. G. (1996). The distinct nature of Chinese capitalism. *The Pacific Review, 9*(3), 426–441. doi:10.1080/09512749608719195.
Ritchie, B. (2010). *Systemic vulnerability and sustainable economic growth: Skills and upgrading in Southeast Asia*. Cheltenham: Edward Elgar.
Ross, M. L. (1999). The political economy of the resource curse. *World Politics, 51*, 297–322.
Sachs, J. D., & Warner, A. M. (1997). *Natural resource abundance and economic growth—Revised*.
Schneider, B. R. (2013). *Hierarchical capitalism in Latin America*. Cambridge: Cambridge University Press.
Small, M., & Singer, J. D. (2006). Correlates of war project: Data sets.
Tanzer, A. (1994). The bamboo network. *Forbes, 154*(2), 138–144.
Thelen, K. (2004). *How institutions evolve: The political economy of skills in Germany, Britain, the United States, and Japan*. Cambridge: Cambridge University Press.
Waldner, D. (1999). *State building and late development. State Building and Late Development*. Ithaca: Cornell University Press.
Weidenbaum, M. L., & Hughes, S. (1996). *The bamboo network: How expatriate Chinese entrepreneurs are creating a new economic superpower in Asia*. New York: Simon & Schuster.
Yeung, H. W., & Coe, N. M. (2015). Toward a dynamic theory of global production networks. *Economic Geography, 91*(1), 29–58. doi:10.1111/ecge.12063.

CHAPTER 3

Thailand: From Autocrats to Oversized Coalitions

The preceding two chapters laid out the theoretical framework I employ to account for variation in economic governance institutions. Chapters 3 through 6 apply the modified varieties of capitalism (VoC) framework to three countries in Southeast Asia. This chapter examines six periods in Thailand's modern history that contain considerable variation in vulnerability and the number of veto players in government.

In the low-vulnerability military rule period of 1957–1973, the Thai armed forces dominated the political scene as a single veto player. Large protests initiated by students from a growing and increasingly vocal urban middle class sparked a chain of events that led to the fall of the military regime in 1973. A period of instability and high vulnerability lasted until 1979, with a succession of short-lived EVP civilian governments and military governments. Finally, in 1979 a semi-democratic civilian-military hybrid regime was created that was able to hold off challenges from the military and parliament during a period of moderate vulnerability. The elections in 1988 ushered in a low-vulnerability period of coalitional government rule, freed of the military's direct supervision. The 1997 economic crisis gutted the government's access to revenues but the post-crisis period was otherwise similar to the one that preceded it, with an EVP government. New electoral rules produced a new government in 2001, dominated by a single party that systematically undermined the ability of other parties to compete. It ruled over a period of low vulnerability until it was deposed in a coup in 2006. Based upon my framework, I expect to observe resulting changes in the policy

J.D. Moore, *Varieties of Capitalism in Southeast Asia*, The Political Economy of East Asia, DOI 10.1007/978-3-319-53700-9_3

Table 3.1 Observations in the Thai case

	Military	*Instability*	*Semi-democracy*	*Coalition Governments*	*Post Crisis*	*Single party rule*
Year	1957–1973	1973–1979	1979–1988	1988–1997	1997–2001	2001–2006
Systemic vulnerability	Moderate	High	Moderate	Low	Moderate	Low
Veto players	Single	Excessive/single	Single (macro), many (sectoral)	Many	Many	Single
Expected policy environment	Mixed/stable	Particularistic/stable	Mixed	Particularistic	Particularistic	Particularistic
Expected economic governance institutions	Mixed	Hierarchical	Mixed	Hierarchical	Hierarchical	Hierarchical

environment and types of economic governance institutions. Likewise, I expect to see patterns in the ways that these institutions came into being, grew, declined, and demised (Table 3.1).

3.1 Military Rule (1957–1973)

3.1.1 Constraints

Veto Power: In 1957, Field Marshal Sarit Thanarat staged a coup d'état against the government of Plaek Phibunsongkhram (Phibun). The following year he centralized control over the Thai state. Sarit's subordinates headed key ministry posts and state enterprises and directed the bureaucracy (Phongpaichit and Baker 1998). Economic policy decisions, both macro and sectoral, followed the junta's agenda. Two factors problematize characterizing the military rule period as a single veto player government: the autonomy of the Finance Minister and factionalism in the military. I shall consider these in turn.

In macro policy, Sarit delegated significant authority to Dr. Puey Ungphakorn, the country's leading technocrat, who served both as Governor of the Bank of Thailand (BoT) and as Minister of Finance. Numerous scholars have noted the importance of Dr. Puey and his autonomy in handling economic affairs (Pongsudhirak 2001; Doner 2009; Muscat 1994; Siamwalla 1997). Tsebelis defines a veto player as an actor whose approval is required for a change from the policy status quo. This concept includes both the institutions that define which actors have this power and the partisan makeup of the actual actors that wield this power. Sarit came to power by means of force of arms and ruled via martial law and an interim constitution that gave him virtually limitless authority. He had opponents in and out of government removed, arrested, or otherwise silenced. In such a situation, any authority granted to a Finance Minister or Bank Governor was completely dependent upon the continued support of the military ruler. Dr. Puey had no actual authority to prevent any policy strongly desired by Sarit or his successor, Thanom Kittikachorn. Neither did he have any ability to pursue any policy that was not favored by them.[1] I argue that, though Dr. Puey asserted considerable influence in crafting economic policy throughout his career, he did not possess veto authority.

Though rifts existed and deepened within the military and between businesses and the military, policy followed Sarit's and later Thanom's preferences. Any collective veto player will have some degree of factionalism, but to be considered an independent veto player the faction must have sufficiently independent power to credibly threaten the position of the rest of the collective player. Competition for rents within the military and the bureaucracy did emerge but no factional interests had sufficient power to challenge the authority of the generals at the top. The Junta put a new constitution into effect in 1968 but the military retained control of policy-making by means of the appointed Senate. The new and short-lived parliament effectively lacked veto power and could do little more than criticize the government and expose corruption. Thanom dissolved it in 1971 by mounting a coup on his own government. Because Thanom largely continued Sarit's programs and represented the interests of a relatively hierarchical military institution, I consider there to be no alternation in veto authority in this period. Thus it is an era with a single, non-alternating veto player.

Systemic Vulnerability: By the time Sarit gained power, Southeast Asia was already a key hot-spot in the global cold war. With communist China so near and violent struggles in neighboring Burma, Vietnam, Cambodia, and Laos, Thailand faced a credible threat along most of its borders. This threat did not diminish greatly over the lifespan of the military government. The budgetary demands created by this threat were alleviated by access to agriculture export revenues and especially to US military aid. Washington quickly judged Sarit as an avid anti-communist and someone it could work with, and funding flowed freely.

There was a substantial Maoist guerrilla network operating in Thailand's rural areas. Made up of farmers and minorities, many of whom resented the intrusive expansion of the central government, these rebels moved to open hostilities in 1965 that reached a peak in 1977 (Phongpaichit and Baker 2004). Though Sarit and much of the military came from rural areas, the junta was not directly dependent on the rural population for continued power and felt limited pressure to consider their concerns when making policy. Massive Bangkok student demonstrations began in 1968 and increased in organization and intensity in the early 1970s, but the junta was likewise willing to give only minimal attention to students' demands. As such, the government did not face the pressure of dividing resources between the country's defense and appeasing a broad coalition of interests.

The unified military period was a case with a single, non-alternating veto player that had a moderate level of systemic vulnerability. Based on the framework developed in the second chapter, we should expect the single veto player to be unhindered by political institutions from maximizing wealth by implementing a particularistic policy platform. However, the constraints posed by moderate systemic vulnerability should provide some limits on both the particularism and the volatility of policy. As such, we should expect to see a mix of hierarchical and coordinated economic governance institutions.

3.1.2 Policy Environment

The framework employed in this book suggests that the policy environment under the unified military period should be only moderately particularistic. That is, it should be evident that those with centralized power limit the use of state policies for personal benefit because of external pressures. As indicated in previous chapters, I differentiate between micro- and macroeconomic policies. Overall, this period plays out as predicted, with a policy environment that was relatively stable and featured broadly targeted policies in some areas but was prone to particularism in others.

Macroeconomic Policy: Macroeconomic policy was both stable and decided by military-approved technocrats that by and large placed economy-wide stability and growth over the interests of any particular firms, families, or cronies. Fiscal and monetary policies were geared toward maintaining a stable exchange rate and avoiding inflation (Muscat 1994). The policy adjustments and fluctuations that occurred over this period were relatively predictable responses to changing external and internal conditions. For example, the government responded to budgetary and current-account deficits in the late 1960s with mild demand-restraint measures, relying on substantial foreign reserves as a cushion (Muscat 1994, 103; Hewison 1989, 106).

The Sarit and Thanom regimes were forced to balance between maximizing particularistic benefits and ensuring overall economic stability. This balancing act was played out in the relationship between the military leadership and Dr. Puey, the senior technocrat.[2] Dr. Puey's task was to achieve the policy goals set forth by the military: stability and growth. But the top brass also sought to enrich themselves and their political supporters in the military. Sarit and Thanom, not being trained in economics, had to rely on conservative technocrats like Dr. Puey to determine how many particularistic policies they could pursue before it endangered overall economic stability and growth (Zhang 2010; Pongsudhirak 2002).

Trade policy was designed to achieve import substitution objectives and maintain government revenues. These goals were also clearly indicated but less consistently followed through on than monetary policy goals. Throughout the Sarit and Thanom governments, tariffs were erected with little economic logic beyond revenue maximization, leading to higher nominal rates of protection on consumer goods than on capital goods and raw materials (Muscat 1994). Inconsistencies in the application of these policies arose in the issuing of exemptions and rebates through sectoral policy. Economic actors making decisions about the specificity of assets they wished to hold faced a stable, mostly untargeted trade policy environment.

Sectoral Policy: While sectoral policy was consistent in its overall approach, it was designed to achieve political as well as economic ends. The upper echelons of the military served as political patrons for wealthy Chinese families. Muscatt notes that the bureaucracy was widely regarded as having failed to achieve the ability to contribute effectively to the public interest outside of a few areas (Muscat 1994, 94). Economic actors making decisions about the specificity of assets they wished to hold faced a stable, particularistic sectoral policy environment. "Corruption and clientelistic networking remained pervasive [in the Sarit regime]…maintaining ties with powerful politico-bureaucrats was still highly valued by business people for such links helped overcome bureaucratic inconvenience or delay and delivered certain privileges and even contracts" (Laothamatas 1992, 31).

Additionally, the Board of Investment (BOI) specifically targeted large, powerful merchant-class families for manufacturing promotion (Suehiro 1989). These large firms were also very well connected to Sarit and the military. "Sarit…held interests in nine companies that obtained promotional benefits from BOI; nine of Sarit's political associates also received BOI status. One source recorded that in 1969 there were 143 government officials or family members who had seats on the boards of 347 firms" (Muscat 1994, 113). Sarit had granted control of sectoral policy to loyal supporters and created a system of uncoordinated and conflicting sectoral policy initiatives.

The scope of these particularistic sectoral policies was bounded by the hard budget constraints imposed by Sarit's technocrats. Thus the military rule period had lower levels of clientelism than in earlier years. "Despite the lack of transparency in sectoral policy and the many incentives for rent-seeking, government–business relations changed in both style and substance after 1960. During this period, clientelism between officials and private firms actually declined. There was increasingly more equality between bureaucratic elites and business, and more formal, policy-based consultation than during the nationalist period" (Christensen 1993, 134).

As expected, the government maintained limits on the extent of particularistic policy. Macroeconomic policy was managed in a relatively predictable manner to achieve broad growth and stability. Size and political clout were prime determinates of BoI promotion but promotional privileges were relatively limited in scope, consisting mainly of tax holidays and tariff exemptions on inputs. In a case with stable, mildly particularistic institutions this framework predicts a mix of coordinated and hierarchical economic governance institutions.

3.1.3 Economic Governance Institutions

Economic governance is expected to be structured in a mix of hierarchical and coordinated institutions in the military rule period. Effective coordination is expected to be limited to issues where interests are relatively harmonious because the availability of particularistic policy benefits will undermine coordinative activities involving distributional conflicts and requiring substantial enforcement.

Corporate Governance Institutions: Corporate governance institutions were mixed between hierarchical and coordinative in the military rule period. Family-centered industrial groups and family-centered financial institutions were the main sources of domestic capital and the key intermediaries for foreign investors. The electronics and electrical industry featured a mix of joint ventures between powerful, diversified family conglomerates and family firms concentrated in that sector.

In the discussion below, I evaluate the relative strength of liberal, coordinated, and hierarchical institutions in order to better track the changing importance of each. In corporate governance, I focus primarily on ownership patterns. The prevalence of widely held firms is evidence of diffuse ownership common in liberal economies. The relative importance of widely held financial institutions or non-pyramidal cross-shareholding in ownership is evidence of patient credit, seen in coordinated economies. The prevalence of diversified family or politically organized conglomerates is evidence of hierarchical economies.

The unattractiveness of widely held firms as a system of corporate governance moving into this period was evidenced by the lack of a centralized, national stock market. Both public and private attempts to create such a liberal market for corporate control met with little success. In 1962 a group of private investors created the Bangkok Stock Exchange (BSE) but the body had limited stock turnover and was not heavily utilized. Even with direct government policies aimed at strengthening liberal corporate governance institutions, private actors did not make use of widely held firms. The Second National Economic and Development Plan (1967–1971) proposed the creation of a sanctioned securities market. In 1968 and again in 1972, the government strengthened its finance and securities regulations. A 1969 plan to create a national capital market, offered by former United States SEC commissioner Sidney Robbins, was commissioned by the Government at the request of the World Bank (Hirankasi 2008). These attempts, both public and private, to initiate a liberal system of corporate governance failed to produce an effective market for corporate control. This failure is consistent with the expectation that the policy environment at the time would make the prospect of holding diffuse assets too risky.

Bank lending was the primary source of external capital throughout the period, making up about a third of financial system assets in 1970 (Unger 1998). But the key Thai banks were dominated by individual families that utilized patron–client and familial ties in the allocation of credit. This led to the expansion of many families into diverse economic activities (Suehiro 1989). The commercial banks grew rapidly in the military rule period (Suehiro 1989). Muscat characterized the behavior of the banks in this period.

> Family governance of commercial banks is generally believed to have exposed a number of Thailand's banks to weaknesses of lending practice and financial stability that would not have occurred if these institutions had been managed by hired professionals along modern corporate lines… Among the problems most commonly cited are the application of looser lending criteria to loans to family members than is the case for arms-length credits to ordinary clients; privileged access for family members to bank credits, during periods of relative illiquidity in the banking system; insufficient diversification of risk because excessively large credits are extended to bank family members; insufficient attention to modernization and professionalization of management. (Muscat 1987)

The Bangkok-based Chinese banking families did, however, engage in some important coordinative corporate governance practices in the agricultural industry. The Thai Farmers Bank and Bangkok Bank in particular were actively engaged in the operations of provincial agri-businesses they provided capital to.

> The banks financed commodity exports, mobilized deposits, and supported firms emerging under import-substitution incentives. Bangkok Bank in particular, because of its dominance – at its peak in the 1960s it garnered approximately 40 per cent of all commercial bank deposits in the country – performed crucial investment coordination tasks...Through investment linkages with agribusiness conglomerates, leading commercial banking families diversified their asset bases and expanded their influence. Most of Thailand's more profitable agro- processors and suppliers of inputs – the feedmills, fertilizer firms, edible oil producers, fruit canneries, meat processors – are large, integrated Bangkok-based firms who maintain strong personal connections with leading commercial banks. (Christensen 1993, 135–140)

Several government lending institutions were created to facilitate greater coordination in finance. In 1959, Sarit's government created the National Economic Development Board and the BoI to organize and coordinate activities in the private sector in the hopes of promoting national industrial growth. The IFCT, it was suggested, could function as a model financial intermediary by demonstrating to "nascent" industrialists the determinants of credit-worthiness (Muscat 1994). In practice, however, the boards distributed most opportunities to family-based conglomerates with powerful military connections. Smaller domestic manufacturers and factory owners that lacked access were excluded.

These powerful, family-controlled commercial banks did not lend much to electrical manufacturers in the military rule period, preferring "trade financing of local merchants through the over-draft system rather than long-term, risky industrial financing of local manufacturers" (Suehiro 1989). Where they did invest in manufacturing, the financial institutions would set up the firms themselves.[3]

In the 1960s, tariff barriers prompted ethnic Chinese merchants that had previously been responsible for selling imported goods to move into production. With the help of foreign partners, they developed large industrial business groups. These groups were mostly initially specialized in a particular industry. Several domestic business groups were important in the electrical sector. As with the financial groups, the industrial groups were centered on families. However, they mainly relied on retained earnings, family resources, and foreign partners for finance. Although authority in these businesses was normally tightly held by the head of the family, many family members would have shares in the enterprise, and all the senior technical and managerial positions would be filled by family members, most often by the founder's sons (Muscat 1994, 116).

Phipatseritham and Yoshihara highlight the importance of access to political authorities for this system:

> In Thailand, if a business family wants to prosper, it is essential to have patrons in the government...power was concentrated in the top echelon of the hierarchy, who ruled the country in a highly personal manner. Thus, not only was the influence of the government on the Thai economy very pervasive, but there was also a great deal of discretion on the part of government official in interpreting rules and regulations...*in Thailand it was very unlikely for a business to become big without entering into a patron-client relationship with those in power*...One source of patronage is the military, which has ruled the country for much of the time during the past several decades. Until the Thanom-Prapass regime fell in 1973, some generals and other high-ranking officers sat openly on the board of directors of a number of companies. In most cases, however, the patrons *could not be easily identified, and contributions to the military for their patronage flowed behind the scene*. Another source of patronage is the Royal Family to whom both the people and the military owe allegiance and who has some influence over government decisions. (Phiphatseitham and Yoshihara 1983, 25–26) [*emphasis mine*]

Inter-firm Linkage Institutions: At the beginning of the military rule period, inter-firm linkage institutions were predominantly hierarchical. Regional and ethnic chambers of commerce had been established in earlier periods but were relatively weak. Partly due to government crackdowns on ethnic Chinese groups in previous periods, these bodies preferred to avoid confrontation and did little to provide unified policy stances to government officials.

There were some direct efforts by the military regime to promote the development of stronger coordinative capacities among inter-firm institutions. The Ministry of Commerce after 1966, provided some promotional privileges specifically to companies that were members of business associations and denied them to non-members. Mostly, however, the government offered encouragement and facilities for offices of new associations. The impact of these policies was not substantial; between 1966 and 1973, an average of only five associations were registered per year (Laothamatas 1992).

Limited public–private consultations were established with some of the existing associations as the newly created National Economic and Social Development Board (NESDB) met with the Board of Trade concerning some policy issues. These too met with limited results, complaining about insufficient revenues from membership fees and a high degree of dependence on the more powerful members. Associations focused on recreation and social functions, by and large unwilling or unable to engage in more challenging coordinative activities such as presenting collective interests to the government, advising officials, or assisting in the supervision of business and trade. The information channels created in these consultations tended to be one way, with associations working as "subsidiary policy instruments" of the government in a type of state corporatism (Laothamatas 1992). Anek makes the link between the particularistic policy environment and limited inter-firm coordination explicit:

> In a society where favoritism and nepotism were more than tolerated, effective clientelistic ties could overcome government-caused inconvenience or delay, and deliver certain privileges and even contracts from the government. In 1969 there were reportedly at least six top politico-bureaucrats each of whom had connections with 20-50 business firms. Another seven influential civilian and military bureaucratic leaders had connections with 10-18 firms each. On the whole, there were more than 80 senior military officers who were each connected to at least one firm. For businessmen then, manipulating clientelistic ties with high officials for their particularistic interests was as important as, if not more important than, lobbying for or against categoric interests. (Laothamatas 1992, 31)

Toward the end of the period, there were discussions of creating a new peak organization with universal compulsory membership and formal government–business consultations but they fell apart in the wake of the 1973 political strife.

3.1.4 *Electrical/Electronic Industry*

This is the period in which local manufacturers in the electronic/electrical industry (EEI) first appeared in Thailand. The policy environment faced by these firms was not appreciably different from the overall policy environment. General price and exchange-rate stability afforded by stable, broadly targeted macroeconomic policy led to a substantial inflow of FDI in the period and created the incentive for local firms to expand into manufacturing. In the electrical industry, sectoral policy largely was implemented via the BoI. Table 3.2 shows BoI promotions in the various subsectors of the electronics and electrical industry. As with other industries, the promoted firms in the EEI represented the largest, and in many cases only, producers in the country at the time. Tariff rates on the electronics industry also reflected the overall import substitution and revenue maximization strategies (Khomate 1997).

The largest initial players in the electrical industry were National Thai, Kang Young Electric Manufacturing, Thai Toshiba Electric, and Sanyo Universal Electric (See Table 3.3). As in other sectors, local companies needed their multinational partners for capital and know-how, but they were not simply subsidiaries. The Thai partners often retained a fair degree of autonomy (Felker 1999, 388). While these Thai–Japanese joint ventures exemplified this trend, there was also one wholly-Thai-owned company, Tanin Industrial.

While all the major Thai JV partners in the EEI were family firms, only Sanyo's Universal Electric had a controlling stakeholder that was

Table 3.2 BoI promotion in the electronics industry

Products	*Number of firms*	*Period of promotion*
Air-conditioner	5	1963–1973
Refrigerator	6	1963–1973
Television	4	1964–1982[a]
Electric fan	5	1965–1978
Radio	4	1964–1982[a]
Telephone set	1	1971–1982[a]
Wire and cable	6	1963–1972
Insulator	2	1975–1982
ICs	7	1973–1982[a]
Compressor	1	1981–1986

Source Board of Investment (Taken from Naronchai 1982)
Note [a]still ongoing as of 1982, the year of publication

Table 3.3 Family firm JV partners in the early electrical industry

	National Thai	*Kang Yong Electric*	*Thai Toshiba Electric*	*Sanyo Universal Electric*	*Thanin Industrial*
JV partner	Matsushita	Mitsubishi	Toshiba	Sanyo	n/a
Thai family	Kanchanachari	Phodhivorakhun	Suriyasat	Mojdara	Vidhayasirinant

extensively diversified across sectors. Maitri Mojdara, an MIT trained engineer, established the Universal Electric Company in 1959, the first Thai company to manufacture electric appliances. It joined with Sanyo and the powerful Osathanukrah family to form Sony Universal Electric in 1969. The Osathanukrahs, who owned a 28% stake in the JV, held one of the Kingdom's largest diversified business empires, with direct interests across the economy (Suehiro 1989; *The Economist* 1977).

The rest of the Thai electronics and electrical JV partners were family firms that had previously served as importers and distributors, with limited holdings outside of the industry. The Siew group was founded by SiewKanchanachari, an ethnic Chinese Thai who had studied electrical engineering in the United States. Siew, who had been the only agent for Matsushita Electric in Thailand since 1954, formed a joint venture with the Japanese giant in 1961, National Thai (51% owner). Initially manufacturing audio products and batteries, the company expanded into the production of new products throughout the military government period, moving into transistor radios (1965), black and white TVs (1967), electric fans and car radios (1968), and finally color TVs (1970). After Siew's death in 1970, the Kanchanachari family retained its critical role as the representatives of the Mastushita corporation in Thailand, with his daughter, Maevadi taking control (*Bangkok Post* 1993).

The Phodhivorakhun family served a similar function for Mistubishi Electric. Sittipol Phodhivorakhun moved to Thailand from Taiwan in 1936 and worked as a sales representative for Mitsubishi electric fans. In 1964 he established Kang Yong Electric Manufacturing as a JV between Mitsubishi Electric Corp. (37% by MEC) to assemble electric fans and other appliances (*Bangkok Post* 1994).

Korn Suriyasat, with an electrical engineering degree from Yale and a group of friends, formed Thai Electric Industries Co. to design and install a/c units and electronics in government buildings, offices, and hotels. They also began producing electrical fans under the 'Sunrise' brand before they started a long relationship with Toshiba Corp. Thai Toshiba Electric was established in 1969 as a joint venture to manufacture table fans. They expanded this to include TVs, rice cookers, refrigerators, water pumps, washing machines, and microwaves.

Tanin Industrial was established in 1962 and began producing black and white televisions in 1965, using imported parts and components. Electronics enthusiast turned importer turned producer, Udom Vidhayasirinum had the only wholly-Thai-owned electronics firm in the country. Though he initially assembled products for foreign brands and moved into producing high-quality radios and television sets, a range of stereo hi-fi equipment, and component parts including electrolytic condensers, volume controls and variable controls and variable condensers, as well as loudspeakers, transformers, coils and printed circuits (*ASSET International (Thai Language)* 1979). Udom Vidhayasirinum noted the inadequacy of promotion efforts for smaller local producers and the difficulty of thriving without partnering with a foreign multinational (The Investor 1972).

These firms were the largest EEI manufacturers with local partners in the military rule period. The Thai partners were all family firms though only Sanyo Universal Electric had a large-scale diversified conglomerate as a controlling shareholder. No widely held EEI firms of any significance existed in this period. Neither, however, did any EEI firms with cross-shareholding arrangements or significant ownership by widely held financial institutions. This is in line with the expectation that the incentives created by the policy environment mildly favored hierarchical corporate governance institutions. The only coordinative corporate governance institution that evolved were with foreign multinational partners, though they tended to be exclusive.

I found no evidence of any significant domestic inter-firm linkage institutions for the electrical/electronic sector in this period. The JVs with multinational firms relied on foreign inputs for their largely assembly operations and used their foreign partners for international distribution. Thanin, the sole wholly-owned domestic firm, also relied on foreign inputs in this early period. No horizontal associations or organizations were created for the EEI. Again, this is consistent with the expectation that when narrowly targeted benefits are available, hierarchical inter-firm linkage institutions should develop. A high degree of dependence on the foreign partner and little contracting or coordinating beyond the bounds of the family relationships in the local partner. As with corporate governance institutions, however, there is less coordination in this period than the 'mixed' outcome predicted.

3.2 Instability (1973–1979)

3.2.1 Constraints

Veto Power: King Bhumibol appointed interim PM Sanya Thammasak and an assembly through consultations with student groups after a mass urban protest turned violent in October of 1973. The government was charged with forming a new constitution and holding elections. As this government was in the process of forming a new set of political institutions, it is unlikely that it would have served as an effective signal to actors deciding whether to hold either co-specific or diffuse assets. The successive two Pramoj governments were large coalition governments, made up of many political parties. There was still the potential for instability and the civilian, elected governments were ultimately taken down by the military, but at the time there was at least a constitution in place and set rules for gaining and sharing power. The successive military governments that followed pushed their predecessors' people out of key positions and installed their own, single alternating single veto player governments. It is unlikely that there was sufficient time for economic actors to feel anything other than uncertainty toward government policies throughout this period. Because of this last reason, I have included 1973–1976 and 1976–1979 within the larger 1973–1979 instability period. That is, according to my theory we would expect that the specific number of veto players would not matter until the underlying level of regime instability decreased.

Systemic Vulnerability: The military threat along Thailand's borders remained real and imminent during its flirtation with democratic rule and throughout the successive military governments. There was no decrease in the pressure to maintain a strong defense force. The communist threat along Thailand's borders was made more acute by the sharp reduction of American forces in the region and support for Thailand.

A combination of largely external factors dramatically diminished the government's revenues and thus its capacity to easily finance continued military spending. Firstly, American assistance dropped significantly, by 36% in 1973 and 44% in 1974 (see Table 3.4). This meant a drop from 1.8% of Thailand's GDP in 1972 to 0.4% in 1974. It never again reached

Table 3.4 US assistance to Thailand US Aid and Military Assistance in millions of US Dollars

Year	*US AID*	*Military assistance*	*Total*	*Percent change (%)*	*Percent of GDP (%)*
1965	19.5	30.4	49.9		1.14
1966	43.8	51.6	95.4	91	1.81
1967	55.3	69.6	124.9	31	2.22
1968	54.2	89.8	144	15	2.37
1969	40.4	96.4	136.8	−5	2.04
1970	33.9	110	143.9	5	2.03
1971	24.0	98.7	122.7	−15	1.66
1972	30.8	122.1	152.9	25	1.87
1973	34.9	62.8	97.7	−36	0.90
1974	19.0	35.4	54.4	−44	0.40
1975	12.9	41.7	54.6	0	0.37

Source US Assistance Data from (Muscat 1990, 295, 328) GDP data from World Bank World Development Indicators

the boom-years of the 1960s. At the same time, the 1973 oil shock led to decreased global demand for Thai agricultural exports, increased cost for shipping, and increased budgetary pressure on the Thai government. Though the US bumped up its assistance to Thailand as it exited, it was not immediately clear that successes in Vietnam would not embolden communist forces. The aforementioned bump in resources was offset by the continued pressure of high fuel prices on government resources (Fig. 3.1).

The massive protests that had led to the fall of the Thanom junta in 1973, had proved that new social forces were mobilizing and that they were well organized. Workers, farmers, and intellectuals maintained a constant pressure on the post-military governments. Royally nominated Sanya Thammasak and the Pramoj brothers headed civilian governments that, lacking clear military backing, relied on public sentiment for their rule. They were thus much more concerned about mass unrest than their military predecessors. Together this made for a period of high systemic vulnerability. The brutality of the '76 massacre drove many left and left-leaning protesters out of the cities. Open conflict with guerrillas continued and though the juntas were not as directly reliant on the support of the people, they were more concerned about maintaining their placidity.

Once the constitution was in place, the unstable rule period featured EVPs and single, alternating veto player governments that faced high systemic vulnerabilities. The framework described in chapter two suggests

Fig. 3.1 World crude oil prices (inflation adjusted USD) *Source* http://www.macrotrends.net

that, though the EVP governments will feel the pressure to maintain a stable, broadly targeted policy environment, they will be unable to overcome the collective challenges to avoiding a particularistic policy environment. On the other hand, the logic implicit in the systemic vulnerabilities approach suggests that the single veto player governments would have been able to limit corruption and maintain policy stability if they had been able to prevent the uncertainty generated by successive coups. Why didn't the high level of vulnerability motivate the military to prevent the potentially disastrous uncertainty generated by the successive changes in government? It is important to remember that the vulnerabilities approach is more evolutionary than (politically) functionalist. That is, high levels of vulnerability will not automatically cause leaders to create the appropriate institutional configurations. Rather, governments which are unable to meet the challenges posed by high vulnerability will eventually cease to exist because of regime change or invasion. There may be some trial and error involved and some states may adjust more quickly than others.

3.2.2 *Policy Environment*

With shifting regimes and sudden changes in the rules of the political game, this framework suggests that the inability of the EVP governments to overcome problems of collective action and the subsequent regime-uncertainty in this period should create a highly particularistic policy environment, despite the systemic vulnerabilities.

Macroeconomic Policy: Macroeconomic policy in this period was uncoordinated and narrowly targeted. The technocrats, who had been insulated by Sarit and Thanom, were suddenly exposed and expected to meet politically motivated ends distinct from stable growth. Thai monetary policy became decidedly expansionary under the civilian administration, with politicians directing the BoT to take a more activist role in expanding the money supply. The benefits were targeted toward particular industries and geographic regions (Muscat 1994). For example, Finance Minister Boonchu established a 'money for transformation' program that allocated money directly to local government (Anuchitworawong 2007; Felker 1999). Significant banking reforms were enacted in 1979, with the purpose of diluting family ownership and limiting the power and discretion of the key banks (Unger 1998). Fiscal policy became much less conservative in this period with money flowing much more freely, with little regard to decreasing revenues. By the end of the period significant imbalances developed (Muscat 1994). Trade policy remained dedicated to maximizing state revenues and protecting powerful firms that had been targeted for promotion under import substitution.

Sectoral policy: Once the civilian administration had gained control over the policy-making apparatus, they were expected to deliver policy benefits to those that had elected them. The dual challenge of reduced US assistance and a massive spike in oil prices meant that the resources previously available to disburse side-payments to supporters was substantially reduced (Muscat 1990, 295, 328). At the same time, the size of the coalition made the creation of a comprehensive system to provide public goods to voters challenging. The result was a highly particularistic sectoral policy environment.

High tariffs combined with case-by-case exemptions favored large, connected firms, across the industrial sector (Narongchai 1982). The BoI continued to provide tax-relief based promotion in the period of instability. Exporting firms were allowed to offset taxes for inputs by applying for exemption status, getting tax rebates after the fact, or using

Table 3.5 BoT rediscounting credit for the electronics industry

Items	*1974*	*1976*	*1978*	*1980*	*1981*
EEI products (Millions of Baht)	11.8	2.7	20.3	290.9	442.7
EEI rediscount as % of industrial products	0.28	0.02	0.13	11.04	11.24
EEI rediscount as % of all products	0.15	0.02	0.09	0.63	0.82

Source BoT and Customs Department (cited in (Narongchai 1982) p. 2.19)

bank guarantees. The BoT also extended a re-discounting credit option to promote exports (see Table 3.5).

The return to power of the military in 1976 meant that close ties to powerful officers was again important. As the military struggled to create an institutional configuration that would, at the same time, allow them to distribute side-payments to an expanded coalitional base and take over a greater share of the military budget from the Americans, the only clear signal they communicated was uncertainty and the continued importance of political access.

3.2.3 Economic Governance Institutions

Economic governance is expected to be hierarchical in the instability period. A combination of regime instability and particularism is expected to prevent economic actors from investing in co-specific assets or diversifying assets in liberal institutions.

Corporate Governance Institutions: Corporate governance institutions remained hierarchical during the period of instability. The Thai capital market grew in fits and starts over the period of regime instability. The 1978 Public Limited Company Act created an ownership structure "in which at least 50% of the total issued shares were to be distributed to a group of shareholders holding less than 0.6% of the total" and was seen as overly restrictive and responsible for deterring companies from going public (Suehiro and Wailerdsak 2004, 86). The 1979 crash of the BSE undermined the limited gains that had been made in the use of open markets for corporate control.

The Thai banking sector became heavily involved with the commercial agribusiness sector in this period (Christensen 1993, 150). The large commercial banks such as Bangkok Bank and commercial conglomerates like Charoen Pokphand each had extensive resources and their own patrons in various levels of government and were able to work together to mutual benefit. The agribusinesses thus helped facilitate some meaningful collective action in that sector. The family firm remained the predominant corporate form in this period and the large Chinese conglomerate remained dominant in industry and banking.

Inter-firm Linkage Institutions: Inter-firm linkage institutions were predominantly hierarchical in this period. The government's nascent program to promote consultation with business associations, started in the military period, was scrapped. The series of short-lived governments "could not afford to formulate any long term, systematic policy, let alone consider various proposals made by leading business associations" (Laothamatas 1992, 32). Once the civilian government was overthrown, the public–private consultations that did occur were few and criticized by business participants that charged that "the government appeared not serious and not sufficiently urgent in implementing any solution advised by the committee" (Laothamatas 1992, 38).

Horizontal, peak industry associations were few in number and generally weak; little was heard of them in the news media of the period (Laothamatas 1992). The Association of Thai Industries (ATI) had a broad cross-section of industry member associations but participation was thin for most of the period. As the end of civilian government meant that the parliament was no longer available as a means for businessmen to influence policy, the latter refocused their efforts on business associations. A loosely organized Joint Standing Committee on Commerce, Industry and Banking was formed and undertook some limited coordination within its membership and across to other associations in the Association of Southeast Asian Nations (ASEAN). This however, did not have a direct, meaningful influence on policy-makers until the semi-democratic period.

The instability period was characterized by hierarchical corporate governance and inter-firm linkage institutions. Coordination declined generally, with public–private institutions scuttled.

3.2.4 Electrical/Electronics Industry

The policy environment facing EEI firms did not differ from the overall policy environment in the instability period. The government continued with high general tariff levels and exemptions distributed by the

BoI, lacking in any overall economic rationale. In the electrical/electronics industry this meant very high tariffs on consumer goods and intermediate parts but generally low tariffs on semi-finished components for assembly (Narongchai 1982). The exemption process was especially complex and costly for EEI firms, involving lengthy assessments by customs officials. Rebates, in the form of future tax credits, were issued on a similarly time-consuming product-by-product basis. Firms wishing to avoid duties on imports to be used as inputs for exports also used bonded manufacturing warehouses to store them. Though popular and used by four EEI firms that produced integrated components (ICs), radios, T.V.s, condensers, automotive air conditioners, and room air conditioners, the customs department was unable to give sufficient personnel resources to meet private demands (Narongchai 1982). The Thai government was also one of the largest buyers of EEI products and was able to provide support to producers by paying 15% higher than market prices for locally produced products. Under Finance Minister Boonchu, the government also began a more explicit industrial policy (Doner and Laothamatas 1994).

Corporate governance remained hierarchical. No significant widely held firms emerged and there were no substantial moves by the major Thai commercial banks into the electronics industry. The earlier relationships between the primary EEI MNCs and local, family-based partners continued through this period, in many cases expanding into new product lines, but there was only one major new domestically owned entrant. The Kamol Sukosol group, a diversified, family-based conglomerate, began manufacturing refrigerators and air conditioners in 1973. Kamol Sukosol, the only child of a wealthy Chinese businessman in Bangkok, started working as an agent for GE in 1939 (Suehiro 1993a). The group's activities were spread across the economy, including automotive, finance, insurance, hotel, and real estate development sectors (Kamol Sukosol Electric Co 2008).

The link between access to particularistic benefits and the large family conglomerates is made explicit by an *Economist* article about tax evasion by Sanyo Universal Electric:

> To the extent that the story has been kept out of the local press for almost two months, there is clearly a degree of local complicity. This is explained by the involvement of one of the country's most prominent and prosperous business families - the Osathanukrohs. It owns 28.4% of Sanyo

> Universal and has wide interests. Recently it negotiated a contract to set up the first arms and ammunition plant in Thailand, manufacturing supplies for the Royal Thai army...Collusion between multinationals, prominent business families, and members of government enjoys a long established tradition in Thailand, and has proved an almost foolproof route to handsome returns on investment. (*The Economist* 1977)

Thus, liberal corporate governance institutions remained weak in this period and no new significant coordinative ventures were established. As expected, the sector was dominated by large, family firms, with another diversified family group as the main new entrant. Inter-firm linkage institutions were likewise hierarchical, with little deep coordination. Toward the end of the period, the EEI Club was established in the Association of Thai Industries, specifically to address the interests and concerns of the EEI sector. Although the club proved to be one of the most dynamic of the ATI (later the Federation of Thai Industries), there is no evidence that it engaged in any intensive coordination at the time of its genesis.

3.3 Semi-Democracy (1979–1989)

3.3.1 Constraints

Veto Authority: The Kriangsak military government established a constitution and oversaw new elections. In 1979, Kriangsak served as PM of an otherwise elected government coalition. The renewed pressures of high oil prices and general unpopularity within sections of the military forced him to step down in 1980 and General Prem Tinsulanonda headed coalition governments for the next 8 years. Once in office, Prem recreated the firewall between macroeconomic management and the line ministries, bifurcating policy along the lines set forward by Sarit. Macroeconomic decisions were deemed critical and insulated from partisan politics. Prem's subordinates were quickly placed in direct control over the powerful Ministry of Finance (MoF) and he effectively held off both military and civilian efforts to steer these policies away from his conservative preferences.

Fiscal policies were enacted by the Minister of Finance, the NESDB, and the Office of the Prime Minister, all of which were accountable directly to Prem (Doner and Laothamatas 1994). The Parliament had no ability to increase the size of the budget, only (in theory) to reduce it. The partisan government coalition partners did fight continuously for control of lucrative government projects once the budget allocation process was complete, but they had almost no say on fiscal policy generally.[4] Monetary and exchange rate policies were mostly decided by the BoT, under the direction of the (MoF). The Finance Minister, able to alter tariff rates without legislative approval, decided trade policies (Doner and Laothamatas 1994).

This means that, though Prem may have delegated policy formation to the bureaucracy (especially the MoF), those institutions represented his preferred policy directions and he served as the sole veto player in macroeconomic issue areas. As this veto authority did not change hands, the framework would lead us to expect the nature of the overall macro policy environment to be determined by the level of systemic vulnerability.

Microeconomic policies, meanwhile, were decided by the elected politicians in conjunction with Prem. The Thai electoral system at this time was an uncommon multi-member multi-vote system that resulted in many small parties.[5] As a result, to form a governing coalition Prem had to bring several parties together. Three governments were formed during his time as PM, each being made up of at least four fragmented political parties. According to Tsebelis each coalitional party may effectively veto a policy by withdrawing from government or threatening to withdraw (Tsebelis 2002). Likewise, Prem had the ability to veto by calling for new elections and reforming the government or threatening to do so. Thus, microeconomic policy changes had to have the approval of the EVPs.

Systemic Vulnerability: The spread of communism throughout Southeast Asia had dominated Thai foreign relations for the preceding three decades and continued to be a pressing concern in the early 1980s. With fears that China, Vietnam, Burma, Laos, and Cambodia would export revolutionary activity, Thailand faced a credible threat along most of its borders. Throughout the decade, however, external threats declined in intensity. Thailand had established diplomatic relations with China and strengthened ties with many of its other neighbors in the ASEAN. Neighboring communist Laos, Cambodia, and Vietnam remained volatile but open hostilities gradually receded over the course of the decade.

The military's coalitional support base broadened beyond the traditional bureaucratic polity system after the social unrest of the 1970s. But Prem's semi-democratic administration broadened it still further, maintaining a keen interest in the degree of mass mobilization. This increase in interest occurred simultaneously with a marked decline in the militancy of the most radical opposition groups in Thailand. The substantial Maoist guerrilla network operating in Thailand's rural areas through the 1960s and 1970s, made up of farmers and minorities, reached a peak in 1977 and had subsequently declined (Baker and Phongpaichit 2014). Student, labor, and farmer activism, which led to the fall of governments in 1973 and 1976 governments, also declined.

A combination of largely external factors dramatically diminished the government's revenues and thus its capacity to easily finance continued military spending. American assistance, which had been a substantial source of revenue, had dropped significantly and never again reached 1960s levels. The 1979 oil shock led to decreased global demand for Thai agricultural exports, increased cost for shipping, and increased budgetary pressure on the Thai government.

Together this makes for a period where initially high systemic vulnerability declined over the course of the decade to an intermediate level. That is, the budgetary demands required to maintain coalitional support were moderately high and budgetary allocations reserved specifically for national defense were high but declining. But at the same time, the resources that filled government coffers were hurt by increased transportation costs and decreased demand. Therefore, according to the framework, we should expect macroeconomic policy to be predictable and broadly targeted initially but subject to a gradual shift toward more narrowly targeted policies. Likewise, we should expect to see strong coordinated institutions early on that gradually give way to mixed coordinative-hierarchical institutions.

As indicated, I differentiate between micro and macroeconomic policy environments. The framework employed in this book indicates that the macroeconomic policy environment, decided by a single veto player subject to high systemic vulnerability, should be predictable and broadly targeted initially. We should expect to find evidence of those with centralized power limiting their use of state policies for personal benefit because of a constrained ability to respond to threatening external pressures. We should expect to see clear tradeoffs between the use of scarce revenues for narrowly targeted side payments and for defense spending—but that particularization of the policy agenda will increase moderately as revenues increase and external threats decrease.

The framework leads us to anticipate that the sectoral policy environment, decided by EVPs, should be highly particularistic. We should expect to see attempts to voluntarily limit particularistic efforts, motivated by the external environment, to fail because of collective action problems. There should be a balkanization of microeconomic policy-making and/or extensive particularistic side payments as part of a log-rolling coalition.

3.3.2 Policy Environment

Macroeconomic Policy: Macroeconomic policy under Prem was both predictable and decided by Prem-approved technocrats that by and large placed economy-wide stability and growth over the interests of any particular firms, families, or cronies. Fiscal policy was consistently conservative and predictable in this period, with the government using hard budget constraints to limit particularism. The government prescribed austerity for the economic ills coming into the decade and followed through on them. It sought an increased role for the private sector to drive growth (Doner and Laothamatas 1994; Niksch 1989).

Monetary and exchange rate policies, decided by the MoF, the BoT, and the NESDB were geared toward maintaining a stable exchange rate and avoiding inflation (Rock 1994). The policy adjustments and fluctuations that occurred over this period were relatively predictable orthodox responses to changing external and internal conditions.

The most substantial macroeconomic policy change in the semi-democratic period was the 1984 un-pegging of the Baht to the Dollar. The move took place in the face of Thailand's worsening trade and balance of payments positions and rapidly dwindling reserves (Vichit-Vadakan 1985). The government had also undertaken two smaller devaluations earlier in the 1980s (Doner and Laothamatas 1994). As such, the widespread expectation that the government would devalue caused a reduction of foreign borrowing, the delay of foreign investments, an increase in capital outflow, and increased imports. Though this expectation was communicated by rumor rather than official channels, it was widespread and based on assessments of earlier policies and the government's overall position such that when the change occurred, it was not a shock.

Trade policy in the semi-democratic period first and foremost was dedicated toward getting the government's fiscal house in order. The tariff rates on the books when Prem came to power were a legacy of earlier import substitution efforts and revenue generation. What was left lacked any real developmental logic and led to higher nominal rates of protection on consumer goods than on capital goods and raw materials (Muscat 1994). Despite some liberalization in the early 1980s, the government's approach to trade policy in the semi-democratic period was relatively consistent. Though Prem's economic team was orthodox, they saw achieving fiscal balance as more important than liberalizing trade. As such, though there were some reforms to trade policy in the Prem years, real rates of protection actually increased. These increases were not, however, designed to nurture infant industries or protect politically powerful domestic actors (Doner and Laothamatas 1994). Additionally, through consultation in the Joint Public Private Consultative Committee (JPPCC), the government was able to keep economic actors informed about any changes and was able to compensate those who stood to lose out with exemptions through the BoI (Laothamatas 1988). Overall, macroeconomic policy was predictable and broadly targeted in the semi-democratic period, as expected.

Sectoral Policy: While sectoral policy was consistent in its overall approach, it was designed to achieve political, in addition to economic ends. Throughout the later part of the bureaucratic policy period and the unstable civilian and military governments of the 1970s, the upper echelons of the military served as political patrons for wealthy Chinese family businesses conglomerates and banks. Though the generals were not immediately supplanted, elected politicians gradually came to dominate the patronage game. The parties that served as part of the coalition governments in the semi-democratic period carved up the cabinet for the positions that provided them with the most patronage opportunities, the Ministry of Industry, Ministry of the Interior, and Ministry of Commerce being the most lucrative (Doner and Laothamatas 1994). Individual parties used the cabinet positions to control individual ministries so that they could divert project-based resources to their clients.

Despite this institutionalized particularization of policy, there is evidence that suggests that there was an overall decline in sectoral policy particularism in this period. There was a decrease in the number of politically powerful individuals on executive boards. A few well-publicized corruption scandals in the period highlighted the degree to which particularistic policy implementation was increasingly looked down upon (Laothamatas 1988).

3.3.3 Economic Governance Institutions

Corporate Governance Institutions: Though corporate governance institutions remained at a predominantly hierarchical absolute level in the semi-democracy period, the trend was for increasingly coordinative institutions. The Stock Exchange of Thailand (SET), having crashed 2 years before General Prem assumed the premiership, was weak at the beginning of the period, with a total market capitalization of only twenty-five billion Baht and seventy-four companies listed. Corporate finance had relied mainly on bank lending, foreign JV partners, and conglomerated family resources (Suehiro 1989).

The formal institutions supporting Thai capital were strengthened during the 8 years of semi-democratic rule. But overall, few domestic firms made use of these liberal corporate governance institutions in ways similar to the Anglo-American archetypes. Strong protections for minority shareholders remained on the books but were poorly enforced (Krishnamurti et al. 2005). The size of the capital market doubled by 1989 but after complex pyramid shareholding structures are taken into account, much of the growth of the capital market was driven by family controlled conglomerates of firms rather than widely held firms (Claessens and Fan 2002).

Thai banks remained the dominant force in finance for the Kingdom at the beginning of the semi-democratic period. Five large commercial banks provided the bulk of domestically sourced external funding for companies. By 1989, Thai commercial banks had 96% of the assets, 98% of the deposits, and 95% of the credit for the overall Thai banking sector. Concentration in these commercial banks decreased in the period (Muscat 1994, 146) but remained overall highly concentrated in size (the top four banks controlling 66.4% of assets, 67.9% of the deposits, and 66% of the credit in 1988) and in ownership (Chaiyasoot 1987). Many of the largest banks remained centered around powerful ethnic Chinese families, despite attempts to reduce concentration.[6] Bank funds continued to move to firms based on familial, ethnic, and political ties rather than an informed assessment of growth potential (Claessens and Fan 2002, 71–103; Suehiro 2001; Suehiro 1993b; Unger 1998). After the liquidity crisis and the resulting increase in BoT and MoF regulatory powers of the mid-1980s, banks increasingly became more directly involved in managing the operations of businesses to which they lent, along the lines of CMEs (Vichit-Vadakan 1985).

Publicly listed firms often had complex pyramid structures of ownership that were ultimately controlled by powerful families. Companies used retained earnings to expand or branch out into new areas and, if they required external funding, they needed access to large banks, powerful family conglomerates, or a foreign partner. Thus, the most critical thing for firms to get and keep capital was not demonstrating short-term profitability or long-term growth capabilities, but rather maintaining access to politically connected individuals and families.

Inter-firm Linkage Institutions: The hierarchical inter-firm linkages that had thrived in earlier periods coexisted with new budding coordinative linkages in the semi-democracy period. The renewed importance of elected politicians clearly made a more direct path for firms to influence sectoral policies toward their own interests in a way that undermined coordinative behavior. According to Anek Laothamatas, "interviews with business leaders revealed that their pattern of election financing, if there is any, is from business people as individuals to candidates as individuals. Thus, an association often has leaders who cultivate relationships with politicians from several parties" (Laothamatas 1988, 456). Party politician BoonchuRochanasathian admitted in 1987 that "when party men contact associations, they look for only short-term, personal benefits…and never devise any policy to develop business associations, or to bring about legitimate party-association cooperation" (Laothamatas 1992, 113).

The drive of individual firms to find their own political patrons continued but did not completely undermine the cooperative capacities of peak associations, and inter-firm institutions grew stronger coordinative capacities through the course of the semi-democratic period. The number of peak business associations grew from 124 business associations in 1979 to 177 in 1987. Membership in the ATI grew from 758 to 1377 between 1981 and 1985. Membership in the Thai Chamber of Commerce also grew from 778 to 1066 between 1980 and 1985 (Laothamatas 1988). The scope of cooperation in these institutions also increased drastically.

> In 1987 almost 200 business associations in Bangkok, mainly in two forms-chambers of commerce and trade associations, were registered with the Ministry of Commerce (MoC). News about their complaints, grievances, and demands were reported regularly in the business sections of news media. A content analysis of PrachachartTurakij, an established semiweekly business newspaper, found that the frequency of reports on

activities of trade associations and chambers of commerce jumped from practically none between 1977 and 1978 to eight per month between 1985 and 1987. From 1979-1981, the early years of "semi-democracy," to 1985-1987 the figures increased about 87%. (Laothamatas 1988)

A JPPCC was formed, at the behest of industry, which met with the government to discuss common concerns. Though this body was overseen personally by General Prem, it was not simply a tool that the government used to control business. Indeed, the organization became a primary pathway for business to deliver requests and complaints to the government. Half of the 34 key issues raised over the course of 46 meetings were forwarded by business directly. Another substantial portion emerged indirectly, in response to earlier business complaints in the venue (Laothamatas 1992, 70). The fact that the BOT was not a key player in the JPPCC, despite previous government efforts to designate the body as the preferred institution to organize diverse industry interests, demonstrates that "the government has allowed the emergence of unofficial peak bodies and a relatively free competition among several peaks" (Laothamatas 1988, 464).

Despite the fact that the JPPCC generally tackled issues where members' interests were relatively harmonious such as reducing red tape, stifling laws and regulations, and excessive taxation, it did undertake some ventures that required more substantial cooperation. Under the auspices of the JPPCC and with the assistance of USAID, the ATI, Thai Chamber of Commerce and TBA developed some collective capabilities including joint research and hiring policy advisors (Laothamatas 1988).

3.3.4 Electrical/Electronic Industry

EEI firms faced the same bifurcated policy environment as existed generally in Thailand during this period. As in other sectors, BoI promotion in the electronics industry was important and tended to favor large, well-connected firms but those state agencies that were directly under Prem's influence attempted to place economy-wide interests ahead of any particular firm or sector. Because of the importance of business associations in this process, I will discuss it in greater detail in the inter-firm linkage institutions section. Some key companies in the electrical sector in this period began establishing cross-shareholding investment patterns coordinated by the BoI.

3.3.4.1 Corporate Governance

Kulthorn Kirby (KK), a refrigeration and air-conditioning compressor manufacturing JV was established in 1980. Managing director Suraporn Simakulthorn described the origins of the company, "the government intended to promote only one producer. So the BoI set a condition that refrigerator makers who use the compressors must also be shareholders in the promoted project" (*Bangkok Post* 1989). The BoI had mandated that downstream refrigeration manufacturers be stakeholders in the project. The final shareholders included: the Simakulthorn Group, the Industrial Finance Corporation of Thailand, Sanyo Universal Electrical Co, Thai Toshiba Electric Industries Co, Hitachi Consumer Products (Thailand) Ltd, Kang Yong Electric Manufacturing Co, AP National Co, FTL Industries Ltd, Admiral Thailand Co, Consolidated Electric Co and KamolSukosol Co; as well as executive director groups of other refrigerator makers. While neither a clear example of Japanese or Korean style cross-shareholding, this ownership structure allowed corporate governance based upon a non-market, coordinative basis. The MNCs and Thai JV partners could develop local, high value-added capabilities to reduce transaction costs and reduce production lead-times.

Over the course of the semi-democratic period, KK entered into JVs with a number of overseas groups to expand production in key components, including rotary compressors for air conditioners with Mitsubishi Heavy Industries Ltd of Japan, thermostats for both refrigerators and air-conditioners with the Ranco Group of the United Kingdom, and electric fan motors used in the air-conditioning industry with Universal Electric Co of the US (*Bangkok Post* 1989).

Similarly, Thai CRT was established in 1989 as a BoI-facilitated JV that included all the major domestic television producers as shareholders. After Tanin Industrial's unsuccessful attempt to develop the capacity to manufacture cathode-ray-tubes, an integral component that made up 40% of the value of color televisions, the BoI and Electrical andElectronic Product Club (EEAIC) worked together to establish a domestic supplier. Siam Cement Group (SCG), one of the largest industrial conglomerates in Southeast Asia, became the main shareholder in the JV. A professionally managed firm that is partially owned by the investment arm of the Thai royal family, SCG then took the lead in finding a foreign supplier of the requisite technology (Suehiro 1989). Though the SCG is directly related to the royal family and is, thus, a form of diversified family firm, it was rather unique as an institutional investor. Suehiro described their role at the time:

> SCG most actively promoted management innovation including group decision-making, a rotating system of executive directors, recruitment of professional managers, and centralized investment plans. Its new management system is quite different from the family-type business which dominates other domestic capitalist groups. As of 1987 there are 8 executive directors at SCG and 18 general managers in the associated firms. Almost all of them were promoted step by step inside the SCG corporate organization…most of them have attained high educational levels. Every manager holds at least a bachelor's degree, and 14 graduated in engineering from Chulalongkorn University. Fifteen also hold master's degrees from institutions in Thailand or abroad. (Suehiro 1989, 244)

Mitsubishi was selected for the project and, at the behest of Siam Cement, became a shareholding participant (Felker 1998). As with KK, since Thai CRT would be the only company given protected status by the BoI, the main downstream TV producers were also made shareholders. Again, a form of corporate governance based on long-term coordinative relationships rather than publicly available market signals or unequal power relations.

The Kanchanachari's Siew group upgraded operations in Thai National, their JV with Matsushita.

> …engineering/R&D activities progressed from cosmetic design changes to standard products, particularly color televisions, to design modifications of components like PCBs, fly back transformers, and deflection yokes for CTVs. The unit also undertook development projects aimed at adapting and improving process equipment to increase productivity. In 1987, the company elevated these engineering activities into a formal R&D unit staffed with eleven engineers. (Felker 1998, 415)

Despite this demonstration of technological capacity and despite direct lobbying, Matsushita opted to invest in a massive expansion and upgrading of high value-added export operations in Malaysia, rather than Thailand. The decision, mainly driven by more favorable terms offered by the Malaysian government, was also influenced by the very successes of National Thai and the Thai electronics sector in upgrading production on their own. Matsushita was apparently more interested in establishing its own network of suppliers with whom it had existing relationships than in risking the technological leakage that might occur by sourcing more value-added, high-technology inputs from wholly owned Thai manufacturers such as Tanin Industrial and suppliers affiliated with their competitors like Thai CRT (Felker 1998; Hatch and Yamamura 1996).

The Mahajak group, a long-time air conditioner importer centered on the Kanchanachayphoom family, formed a JV with Mitsubishi in 1988 to produce air conditioners. Mahajak was involved in other sectors of the electronics industry. New JV firms were also created in this period, including GoldstarMitr, Thai Samsung Electronics and Siam NEC (Techakanont 1997). A number of medium-sized Thai firms were also established that imported and assembled completely knocked down units for the domestic market. These included Caren Somboon Industry, Chai Wanee, and TRI-star Industry.

The economy-wide trend toward stronger non-market, non-hierarchical inter-firm linkages was reflected in the electrical/electronics industry. Specifically, the Federation of Thai Industries (FTI) Electrical and Electronic Product Club (EEAIC) took an increasingly active role in promoting and intermediating between the interests of its member firms. The FTI contracted with Chulalonkorn University to "conduct research on the tax structure of the electrical and electronic appliance industries for presentation to the government" (Laothamatas 1988, 457). The effort "resulted in a reduction of import duties on electrical and electronics goods and on certain inputs used in the production process according to the tariff notification of November 26, 1987 issued by the Ministry of Finance" (Amonvadekul 1989, 60).

The National Electronics and Computer Technology Center (NECTEC) was established under the Ministry of Science, Technology and Energy in 1987. The center was created to support R&D in the electronics industry. By the end of the semi-democracy period it had developed many prototypes, including: small electric motors, VLSIs, electronic timing devices, automatic Thai–English data preparation, a microcomputer hardware training and development module and national budget preparation software (*Bangkok Post* 1989). Additionally, the downstream firms in the refrigerator, air conditioner, and television industries were able to overcome competitive interests and promote supplier development in key areas. The Air Conditioning and Refrigeration Club was established within the FTI in 1979 and, like the EEIAC, proved to be an important associational venue for the players in the industry.

As noted in the section on corporate governance, the BoI initiated a supplier development program in the refrigeration industry during the semi-democratic period, requiring a corporate governance structure which stipulated that affected downstream firms must to stakeholders in the project. The novel ownership structure, however, did not completely prevent defection among the downstream firms. Sanyo Universal Electric, the Thai JV between Sanyo and the powerful Thai Osathanugrah and Mojdara families, used their political connections to gain permission to bypass KK's monopoly. The Osathanugrahs had a family member serving as the Minister of Commerce in the Prem administration representing the Social Action Party; he was forced to resign in a scandal for permitting logging imports from Burma in 1986 (Neher 1988). Sanyo Universal Electric began producing condensers for refrigeration units in 1983, getting special permission from a Deputy Minister for Industry. The Australian government, on behalf of Kirby (The Australian partner in the project), approached Prem on an official visit and raised the violation of KK's BoI promotion. Though Sanyo's project was not stopped, KK was granted an additional 3 years of promoted status (Fletcher and Barrett 2001; Fletcher 2001).

Another promotional problem occurred when SCG and Mitsubishi endeavored to gain BoI promotion for their proposed rotary condenser production JV in 1987, again violating the terms of KK's promotion. In the end, the BoI granted the JV promotion but KK also entered into a new JV with Mitsubishi to produce rotary condensers (Jiji Press English News Service 1987; *Bangkok Post* 1989). Again the matter was sent to the PM's office to resolve.

In 1985 Thai television manufacturers and members of the EEAIC of the FTI decided to initiate a project to produce cathode-ray-tubes (CRT) for use in TV exports. The EEAIC was one of the most active FTI clubs, serving as a coordinating point for the powerful Thai families that had been involved in joint ventures with foreign electronics producers (Felker 1998). These family groups had both common and conflicting interests, just as they were both allied with and opposed to their foreign MNC partners. The group's decision to promote supplier development in CRTs was bolstered by a FTI-commissioned Chulalongkorn University technological and economic feasibility study on the idea. The results indicated that local demand would only justify one local CRT producer and that government protection would be required for the project to be successful.

The group submitted the plan to the BoI for promotion consideration in 1986. The BoI found the project appealing because of the 800 million Baht in foreign exchange saved each year and the potential to create 1100 jobs (*Bangkok Post* 1989). Initially, the board required that the project be locally owned and managed. In negotiating the details of the initiative, the EEAIC was well aware of the distributional implications. To ensure that the project was fair to the membership (downstream TV assemblers), they decided that a trusted, neutral partner with considerable resources was required to implement it. SCG met these criteria, having no direct interests in the TV industry, a reputation of professionalism, and the backing of the wealthy and well-connected Crown Property Bureau.

The SCG formed its own feasibility assessment group and convinced the downstream assemblers to jointly invest in the project (see Thai CRT section of Corporate Governance Institution section for more on ownership). It also wanted one of the main TV MNCs to be directly involved in the project and own a significant stake, in opposition to the BoI's initial requirement that it be a Thai endeavor. They compromised and required that the technology provider also own a substantial stake in the firm (Felker 1998). Nine foreign producers offered to join and Mitsubishi Electric Corp. was selected.

3.4 Coalitional Governments (1989–1997)

3.4.1 Constraints

Veto Authority: Excepting the brief, appointed governments of the 1991–1992, the pre-crisis parliamentary period was one with many players sharing veto authority over macroeconomic and microeconomic policies. Control of this authority changed hands frequently. As noted above, the multi-member multi-vote electoral system led to small, fragmented parties and consequently large coalition governments. The new civilian governments were fragile coalitions of political parties that were also unstable internally. Rural businessmen created geographically based electoral machines which formed the basis of powerful factions which migrated from party to party, seeking to remain in government. These figures used pork distribution, loyalty ties, and vote-buying to deliver large blocks of votes to the party that promised to deliver the most lucrative government appointments and contracts (McVey 2000). Thus, the already large number of veto players was expanded significantly by the institutionalized factionalism that guaranteed these smaller, non-party groups effective veto power (Table 3.6).

Table 3.6 Size of coalition governments in the coalition democracy period

Years in power	*Number of parties*	*Names of parties*	*Prime Minister*
1989–1990	5	Chart Thai, Social Action Party, Democrats, Chatichai Rasadorn, and United Democrats	Chatichai
1990–1991	5	Chart Thai, Solidarity, Prachakorn Thai	Chatichai
1992–1993	5	Democrats, New Aspiration, Palangdhama, Solidarity, Social Action	Chuan
1993–1994	5	Democrats, New Aspiration, Palangdhama, Solidarity, Seritham	Chuan
1994–1995	5	Democrats, Palangdhama, Solidarity, Seritham, CCP	Chuan
1995–1996	7	Chart Thai, NAP, Palangdhama, SAP, Nam Thai, Prachakorn, Muan Chon	Baharn

With the military no longer able to shield the macroeconomic policy bureaucracy, the elected members of parliament rapidly took control of the relevant ministries (Unger 1998). Now, the entire economic policy system was decided by the coalition governments. Fiscal policy was still decided by the MoF. The Chatichai government rapidly sidelined the NESDB and the other bureaucratic agencies that had kept the budgetary process out of the hands of the party politicians under Prem. Before, the coalition partners fought over project allocation once the size of the overall budget was handed down by the technocrats. Now, they were free to increase the budget, subject only to coalition approval.

Monetary and exchange rate policy continued to be decided by the BoT under the MoF. But this technocratic institution was also made more directly accountable to the coalition government (Unger 1998). Trade policy was decided by the Finance Ministry. Thus macroeconomic policy was decided by coalitions with a minimum of five highly fractured parties. Sectoral policy continued to be run from both the technocratic institutions under the MoF and the line ministries. But the elected ministers of parliament put significant pressure on the previously autonomous bodies. The result was EVP governments. The regular patterns of coalition formation, crisis, and reformation throughout the period cycled the parties and factions that held particular offices.

Systemic Vulnerability: Thailand had low levels of external threat during this period. The global communist threat decreased further with the fall of the Soviet Union. Thai relations with China continued to improve and any threats posed by the Indochinese communist states were contained and much more limited in scale and scope.

The coalition governments of this period represented a wide cross section of the Thai population. Parties and factions formed patron–client networks and were able to buy votes and otherwise subvert the democratic institutions but these methods were only successful when the voters were otherwise docile. Leaders had to ensure that pork and patronage flowed to voters and could not afford to completely ignore their interests (Baker and Phongpaichit 2005; Phongpaichit and Baker 2000; Hicken 2006). Though protests again proved important in ending the brief Suchinda government, they were middle class, single issue protests concentrated in Bangkok and lacked a wider mass-base.

While the value of agricultural exports declined relative to the size of the economy, the fall in oil prices eased pressure on government resources and boosted global demand. The boom of the late 1980s continued into the early 1990s and increasing government tax revenues was the trend. According to my argument, the EVP governments of this period should have been sufficient to produce a particularistic policy environment and a hierarchical set of economic governance institutions.

3.4.2 Policy Environment

The framework employed in this book leads us to expect that the policy environment in the coalition government period would be highly particularistic. Any stability gained by the inability of the many veto-player coalitions to change laws through formal parliamentary channels ought to be undone by a similar inability of the governments to monitor policy implementation. The resulting balkanization of the government into ministerial fiefdoms, led by rotating political parties and shifting factions, means that there is no institutional constraint on the ability of the ministers to gain as much individual and partisan benefit as possible from public office. As such, we should expect the policy environment to be highly particularistic.

Though fiscal policy was overall much less predictable than in the semi-democratic period, government spending rose consistently throughout the coalitional period. The annual budget was officially determined by the MoF but coalition parties and factions were able to demand spending increases. Direct control of the MoF had some impact on the rate at which spending increased but fiscally conservative Finance Ministers proved generally incapable of reigning in coalition partners. The rest of this section will follow the policy environment under each of the elected coalitional governments in this period.[7]

Chatichai. PM Chatichai Choonhavan's first Finance Minister, Pramual Sabhavasu, enjoyed an independent factional power-base within the PM's Chart Thai party and favored an expansionary budget (*Bangkok Post* 1989). The budget grew past what Prem had previously allocated for the first fiscal year of the civilian government to an overall 17% increase over the previous year, with the highest spending increase in a decade. This was followed by another 17% increase the following year. In August, 1990, Pramual was replaced by Virabongsa Ramangkura, who was much more technically qualified. Virabongsa, well known for his support for fiscal conservatism, signaled more restraint in the government. Thai Bankers' Association president Pakorn Thavisin's comments after Vibongsa's appointment typify the view that fiscal policy is a function of the persons in charge of the Ministry, rather than any coherent government agenda: "I think there would be a number of changes in both fiscal and monetary policies under this Finance Minister, particularly with policies involving banking" (*Bangkok Post* 1990). But coalitional pressures quickly forced Chatichai to reshuffle again in December, replacing the conservative technocrat with Chart Thai Secretary-General Banharn Silpa-archa. Opposition Democrats criticized the government for Banharn's actions to personalize control of the Ministry by sidelining Deputy Finance Minister Chavlit Thananchanan—assigning him to other duties. "The assignment shows Mr. Banharn will control the country's fiscal and monetary policy by himself. It is very dangerous for the country's economic stability because Mr. Banharn is not an economist and does not intend to respect the opinion of technocrats" (*Bangkok Post* 2000). Banharn also served only briefly as Finance Minister before he was removed following the 1991 coup.

Exemptions to official taxes were distributed by multiple sources and safeguards on implementation were generally lax. The Chatichai government promised to pursue a significant overhaul of the business tax system, from a consumption tax, which often double or triple-taxed companies, to a value-added tax. Year after year the government delayed the implementation of the switch, citing widespread business and popular uncertainty about the plan. The 1990 ejection of the Democrat Party, which supported the reform, was followed by a reduction of the government's resolve in following through with it. The Democrats subsequently criticized Finance Minister Banharn for not being clear on whether the government would follow through on the VAT structure. The military-appointed Anand government put the issue to rest in 1991 by finally adopting the VAT system.

Tax exemptions for industry in general and electrical producers in particular were provided by the BoI throughout the period. As with earlier periods, BoI promotion privileges were highly skewed toward large firms, who also tended to have substantial political connections. PM Chatichai suggested ending the privileges and the Board all together but faced fierce opposition to the suggestion by coalition partners and industry (including then FTI head and future PM Anand Panyarachun).

Monetary and exchange rate policy continued to be decided by the BoT under the MoF. But this technocratic institution was also made more directly accountable to the coalition governments (Unger 1998). EVP government pressures limited the predictability of the policy environment. Finance Minister Pramual, who came from a powerful faction of PM Chatichai's own Chart Thai party, pursued an expansionary monetary policy, even when the PM and his advisors were pushing for higher interest rates. He sidelined and then replaced the governor of the BoT for advocating more restraint. He also started a campaign against powerful banking institutions in a bid to liberalize the financial system. Virabongsa, Pramual's replacement and a respected technocrat, allowed the BoT to act with greater independence and interest rates were subsequently raised. PM Chatichai was removed in a coup in February of 1991. Parliamentary rule resumed in 1992 with the election of Chuan-Leekpai.[8]

Chuan I. The return of elected government in 1992 brought in a widely respected economic team. The new Minister of Finance, Tarrin Nimmanhaeminda, had just resigned as president of Siam Commercial Bank, and was joined in the government by fellow banking luminaries Deputy Prime Ministers Amnuay Virawan and Supachai Panitchpakd. But there was considerable uncertainty over which of these economic technocrats, who held differing visions of an appropriate fiscal policy, would end up controlling policy, and there was no sense that decisions would be clearly directed from the top. To this ideologically grounded source of policy unpredictability was added the usual partisan sources. Right off the bat, the newly elected government sent mixed signals about its 1993 budget, with BoT Governor Vijit Supinit and FM Tarrin openly championing a balanced budget and Deputy PM Boonchu (of the Palang

Dharma party) trying to keep the option clear for deficit spending. When the budget was finally set, there was indeed a significant spending increase and a deficit. Tarrin attempted to modify the budget allocation process and keep the MoF in charge but his efforts had little impact and coalition partners continued to divert large amounts of funds to their constituencies from the 1994 and 1995 budgets.

The bulk of government spending went to large infrastructure investment and constituency pork. Spending was targeted to industry in general and the electrical industry in particular was narrowly targeted.[9]

Banharn and Chavalit. Chart Thai Party's Banharn assumed the PM position in July of 1995, after a series of scandals rocked the Democrat-led coalition. PM Chavalit's government came to power in December 1996, with a stellar 'dream team' of economic technocrats led by Finance Minister Amnuay and BoT Governor Rerngchai Marakanond. Amnuay sought to reign in government spending and counter systemic problems in the financial sector. The significant cuts were shot down, however, as specific projects targeted for trimming were defended by factional interests within the ruling coalition (MacIntyre 2003a, b). A stagnating economy meant lower tax revenues, which made the need for spending cuts even greater, so that Amnuay's planned orthodox monetary policy measures could proceed. The specific factions and parties that stood to lose from the cuts resisted and the budget trimming that resulted was too little and too late. Eventually, to appease his coalition partners, Chavalit sided with the elected politicians and accepted Amnuay's resignation.

As with fiscal policy, monetary and exchange rate policies were narrowly targeted under Chavalit—despite the high profile technocrats in his administration. Major problems in the Kingdom's financial architecture were clearly visible by the start of the Chavalit administration and cleaning up the failing finance sector was one of the major projects set aside for the technocrats in the MoF and BoT. But again, efforts to restructure the whole of the financial system were undermined by individual parties and factions seeking to protect their particular interests. In March of 1997, Amnuay and Rerngchai halted trading of financial companies on the SET and announced that all banks and finance companies would have to make "stronger provisions for bad debt" and that the 10 weakest financial companies would have to "raise their capital base" (MacIntyre 2003a, b). The move was scuttled by Chart Pattana, one of the coalition partners, whose leading members had controlling interests in some of the 10 targeted financial institutions.

Because letting the weak financial institutions fail had systematic repercussions, the BoT ended up spending vast sums propping them up. The resulting increase in the money supply (worsened by the fact that it had been unable to limit the government's fiscal excesses) forced the Bank, which was unwilling to surrender the peg to the Dollar, to spend its foreign reserves to maintain the Baht's value. Thus, in effect, monetary and exchange rate policies were held hostage to the particularistic interests of the coalition parties and factions. Amnuay's replacement Thanong Bidaya, faced a similar roadblock when he sought to suspend 16 finance companies. Chart Pattana leaders prevented its implementation. Again, in August, while one arm of the government sought to reign in and clean up the financial sector, another undermined it, with the Association of Finance Companies lobbied Chart Pattana leaders and the PM directly to relax requirements. MacIntyre notes the dynamic, "Even if a majority were in favor of taking action, a minority that was prepared to play hard ball could veto the action by threatening to walk out of the coalition" (MacIntyre 2003a, 99).

The primary tools of industrial policy in the coalitional period were tax exemptions and holidays, as discussed in the previous sections. With the elected politicians freed to expand the size of the budget as well as determine its distribution, sectoral policy expenditures expanded. Funds were directed, in the form of pork projects, to the political machines of legislators throughout the period (Wong-Anan 1994). In addition to direct promotion of companies in the BoI, the government initiated a number of programs that targeted whole sectors and were, on the face, designed to overcome market failures. On the whole, they were little utilized in practice as competing ministerial interests and initiatives undermine the effectiveness of the programs.[10]

3.4.3 Economic Governance Institutions

Corporate Governance Institutions: Corporate governance institutions remained predominantly hierarchical in the coalition government period. Although powerful families increasingly relied on growing capital markets to secure funding, pyramid shareholding schemes ensured a strong binding of ownership and control. Banks continued to be an important source of finance, but as with earlier eras, lending decisions were based

Table 3.7 Firm ownership in Thailand (1996)

Type	*Percent (%)*
Widely-held	6.6
Widely-held corporation	15.3
Widely-held financial	8.6
Family	61.6
Other	8

Source (Claessens et al. 2000)

more along political and familial ties than according to credit-worthiness. The trend over the coalition government period was for the incentives created by the policy environment to override and undermine the intended effects of statutory reforms. Interestingly, many of the coordinative corporate governance institutions that emerged in the semi-democratic period flourished in the boom years of the coalitional government period.[11] Table3.7 shows the actual breakdown of firm ownership just before the 1997 crisis.

Commercial banks were a major source of external finance at the beginning of the coalition period. Outstanding commercial bank credits totaled 1479 billion Baht in 1990, with over a quarter of total lending going to manufacturing (Sirivedhin 1998; Chaiyasoot 1987). Banking was also highly concentrated, with the four largest commercial banks holding 66.4% of the total assets, deposits, and credits extended. Though by the early 1990s, some of the largest banks had increased the role of professional management, each was still by and large controlled by single families. Large firms were disproportionately the recipients of bank credit and family and political ties tended to trump creditworthiness when lending decisions were made.

The capital account liberalization that occurred as a consequence of the 1992 Anand government's reforms dramatically increased the availability of foreign credit in Thailand. The Bangkok International Banking Facilities (BIBF), introduced in 1993, became the entry point for foreign lending. In large part due to the BIBF, "the outstanding amount of commercial bank credits has risen sharply…to Baht 4300.9 billion in 1995" (Sirivedhin 1998, 208). About 90% of BIBF lending was used to finance productive sectors such as exports, manufacturing, and trade and investment. Thus this large expansion of foreign capital was channeled through the hierarchically organized banking institutions.

The coalition period featured a significant expansion of the formal liberal corporate governance institutions. These formal institutions were, however, largely altered to meet the needs of private actors whose incentives were still primarily driven by the hierarchical policy environment. Thailand's capital market, the SET was already 25 billion Dollars in 1989 and reached a peak of 141 Billion Dollars in 1995. "Total external financing of Thai enterprises as a percentage of GDP rose from 15.7% in 1989 to 26.9% in 1995. As observed by Callen and Reynolds, between 1980 and 1990 about two-thirds of investment is estimated to have been financed by internal funds. In 1991–1995 the ratio fell to one-third" (Sirivedhin 1998, 207).

Family-centered commercial banks remained the dominant feature of corporate governance institutions during this period. In the 1990s, already powerful Thai banks were able to secure funding from various sources worldwide. Though a few of these banks adopted more professional management styles, lending practices still favored access over other factors. Banks or banking families owned many of the new financial institutions. Thus, as with the semi-democratic period, the strongest corporate governance institutions were hierarchical.

Inter-firm Linkage Institutions: Some of the nascent coordinative inter-firm linkage institutions that emerged in the semi-democratic period gradually declined in the coalition government period. Other, new institutions, both private and public–private, were created but cooperation was shallow. The number of business associations continued to grow but they did not succeed in activities or initiatives that required extensive coordination.

> The exit of the non-elected elements-Prem and the technocrats in the cabinet-has created more opportunities for influential businessmen to present their problems, grievances, and demands (especially ones that are particularistic, as opposed to group-based) through political parties and politicians, rather than through the JPPCC system. Some knowledgeable political observers even believed that politicians in power have deliberately toned down the importance of the central JPPCC in order that they may pursue the politics of spoils and patronage more effectively. (Laothamatas 1992, 74)

The main peak industrial association, the Federation of Thai Industries, was seen as politically ineffectual at presenting the collective interests of manufacturers. "During the early '90s, the FTI was regarded as little more than a gentlemen's club with little policy input at government level. Thailand's main conglomerates, although nominal members, preferred to use their own individual lobby channels" (Cheesman 1998). As mentioned earlier, several government initiatives were created to improve vertical inter-firm linkages. The BoI Unit for Linkage Development (BUILD) was created specifically to encourage stronger relations between suppliers and producers but participation was limited and the program lost steam (Ritchie 2002; Lauridsen 2005).

3.4.4 Electrical/Electronic Industry

In the first half of the period, the Thai commercial banks had only limited interests in the electronic and electrical appliance industry. One of the first banking entrants into electronics manufacturing was the Nakornthon Bank, owned by the powerful Wanglee family. In 1988, the family provided funding to a young entrepreneur in the integrated circuit (IC) industry named Charn Uswachoke. Charn describes how he gained access to the loans necessary to start his business, "I got an introduction through a friend of mine who was an executive at their bank. They did not understand the electronics business well and they also are very conservative. But they looked at me and trusted me and believed in me" (Financial Times 1996). Charn's Alphatec Electronics immediately took over Thai operations of Signetics from Dutch Phillips, with Phillips guaranteeing to purchase 90% of the output over the next 5 years. The company began production in 1991 and went public in 1993 using the influx of investment to gain more loans from the key Thai banks. In the same year, Charn acquired a semiconductor assembly plant from National Semiconductor, telephone production and testing plants from AT&T, and moved upstream into the tool and plastic die industry (Fagan et al. 2001).

In 1994, awash with BIBF credits and looking for promising investments, several of the main banking families turned their eyes to the electronics industry (*New York Times* 1994). Using his close ties to the powerful Wanglee family, Charn was able to gain access to the most powerful banking families in the Kingdom (Fagan et al. 2001). These ties resulted in an astounding 800 million Dollar loan to finance Charn's wafer project. Charn himself describes the importance of personal ties in the loan-approval process: "The details are left to other people. They are just a formality. In principle they have agreed to lend to us and in Thailand we keep our word, our promise. Some people might have a problem with the banks but you have to get to know the people at the top level and then it's easy. We do business here from the top down" (*New York Times* 1994).

As with banking in other sectors in earlier periods, the loans and overdrafts provided to Alphatec in this period were not based on a strict assessment of credit worthiness. Unlike similar investments by powerful banking groups in the European CMEs, these loans came with limited oversight and control on behalf of the banks.

The cross shareholding structures (Thai CRT and Kulthorn-Kirby) set up in the semi-democratic period continued to expand both vertically and horizontally in the coalition period, strengthening their linkages with their various MNC shareholders. Kulthorn Kirby began producing compressors with a new rotary technology in a JV with Mitsubishi and Aichi in 1988, with Thai companies holding 60% equity in the venture (*Bangkok Post* 1989a). They moved upstream, creating the Kulthorn Kirby Foundry Co. to produce casting and Thai Sintered to produce powdered metal products for both domestic condensers and auto parts (Kulthorn Group 2009a, b). KK took the lead in JVs to produce thermostats with Ranco and to produce fan motors with Universal. KK increased their capital in 1990 (a 63 million Baht increase) and 1993 (a 70 million Baht increase) (*Bangkok Post* 1990). In 1995 it secured a 250 million Baht loan from the Industrial Finance Corporation of Thailand.

Thai CRT was performing well and had initiated a move into computer monitor production when the crisis struck (Changsorn 1998). Though the already-established cross shareholding firms thrived in this period, no significant new similarly structured firms were created.

Again following the trend, Charn's Alphatec Electronics' access to capital flows were no more based on 'publically available information about the firm's profitability' than his access to banking finance was based on credit-worthiness and a controlling stake in the firm's activities. One of the firm's directors highlighted the board's lack of concern about their fiduciary responsibilities, "We trusted Khun [Mr] Charn, so the board never questioned what he had invested in" (Backman 1999). Alphatec's pyramidal corporate structure became evident in the wake of the downturn in the semiconductor sector and the economic crisis:

> Big losses were concealed with big borrowings: at least two sets of books had been kept; false profits of 164 million Dollars had been reported between 1995 and April 1997, when in fact the company's true results were losses; 127 million Dollars had been lent to 'related persons' – companies privately held by Charn – without the permission of the board; recorded revenues were between six and ten times as high as they actually were; funds had been shifted between companies to bolster accounts to attract loans and orders; and invoices had been faked to support fictitious transactions…Other suspicious trades between Alphatec Electronics and companies wholly owned by Charn were also detected. One subsidiary had generated US 50 million Dollars in its first year, but struggle to remain profitable thereafter under the weight of more than US 40 million Dollars in loans had made in less than a year to support the Uswachoke family's private companies (Backman 1999, 30). (Backman 1999)

More local companies moved into the booming electronics and electrical appliance sectors as suppliers during this period. The corporate governance institutions of these firms largely reflected the national patterns. As described above, though Alphatec Electronics utilized substantial bank loans and capital investment, corporate governance was pyramidal and centered on Charn's family.

Far more than the FTI generally, the Electrical and EEAIC and the Air Conditioning and Refrigeration Club continued to be important venues for the powerful firms in that sector to coordinate their activities. It is important to note, however, that Charn's Submicron project went directly to the Thai financial institutions and foreign partners with no real engagement of the EEAIC.

In the electronics sector, NECTEC's promise as a focal point for the industry was never realized and it ultimately became concerned predominantly with political lobbying (Ritchie 2005). Aside from its director's close relationship with the Submicron endeavor, the body was seen as disconnected from industry. For example, in 1997 the EEAIC criticized a NECTEC plan for moving into high end products and sought greater input into NECTEC's decision-making process (Priwan 1997).

Overall, the coalitional government period produced no substantial new EEI firms with coordinative corporate governance, though those that had been created in the semi-democratic period remained. Inter-firm linkage institutions were limited and engaged in little in-depth coordination.

3.5 Post-Crisis (1997–2001)

3.5.1 Constraints

Veto Players: The electoral system that had produced the large coalitions common in the first half of the 1990s was still in place until 2001. The pattern of government formation, scandal, and reformation continued, producing shifting coalitional control of particular ministries. The Democrat and Chart Thai political parties struggled to form coalition governments after the fall of the Chavalit government. Ultimately, the democrats formed a coalition of six highly factionalized political parties (Punyaratabandhu 1998). After land and health care scandals and an unfavorable court decision in 1998 the coalition brought in opposition party Chart Pattana (Far Eastern Economic Review 1998; Reuters News 1998a, b). More scandals and the removal of the Social Action Party from the coalition brought a reshuffle in 1999. The size and makeup of coalition governments in this period are listed in Table 3.8.

Systemic Vulnerability: While no new external threats emerged in this period, the crisis brought a significant increase in mass unrest and decrease in state revenues. The austerity measures enacted as part of conditionality attached to stabilization loans together with the massive 'fire-sale' on Thai stocks and assets produced a large increase in protests (Punyaratabandhu 1998, 1999). Protests expanded as unemployment grew and the government was under substantial pressure to use state revenues to reduce unrest.

From 1997 until the new constitution's electoral rules produced a radically different partisan environment in 2001. Thailand had an excessive number of veto players and a moderate-high level of systemic vulnerability. Again, the presence of EVPs should be sufficient to produce

Table 3.8 Size of Coalition Governments in the Post-Crisis Period

Years in power	*Number of parties*	*Names of parties*	*Prime Minister*
1997–1998	6	Social Action Party, Chart Thai, Solidarity, Chart Thai, Prachakorn Thai, Democrats	Chuan
1998–1999	7	Social Action Party, Chart Thai, Solidarity, Chart Thai, Prachakorn Thai, Democrats, Chart Pattana	Chuan
1999–2000	6	Chart Thai, Solidarity, Chart Thai, Prachakorn Thai, Democrats, Chart Pattana	Chuan

a particularistic policy environment and hierarchical institutions—despite the pressures created by the crisis.

3.5.2 Policy Environment

The framework employed in this book leads us to expect that the policy environment in the post-crisis period would be highly particularistic. Any stability resulting from the inability of the many veto-player coalitions to change laws through formal parliamentary channels ought to be undone by a similar inability of the governments to monitor policy implementation. This should hold despite the increased vulnerability caused by the economic crisis. The resulting balkanization of the government into ministerial fiefdoms, led by rotating political parties and shifting factions, means that there is no institutional constraint on the ability of the ministers to gain as much individual and partisan benefit as possible from public office. As such, we should expect the policy environment to remain highly particularistic.

Macroeconomic Policy: As expected, macroeconomic policy remained highly particularistic in this period, with proposed post-crisis reforms largely undermined by the balkanized government. By the time the Chuan government came to power in November 1997, the political machinery responsible for formulating monetary and exchange rate policies were widely held responsible for the deepening of the crisis. In April of 1998, the Chuan government appointed Chatu Mongol Sonakul as the Bank Governor and tasked him with restructuring the internal workings of the BoT. The Monetary Policy Committee and the Financial Institutions Policy Board committees were established to focus on each of the bank's main functions and balance the power of the Bank Governor (Satitniramai 2007). The reformation was completed but not legally sanctioned. The BoT also sought to reduce the considerable power that the Minister of Finance had over their decisions. They introduced a draft amendment that would end the Minister's ability to dismiss the Governor and require that 60% of the Upper House of the Parliament agreed to such a move. The government ignored the Bank's position and attempted to strengthen the MoF's position relative to the BoT by interfering with their accounting practices in a way that softened the government's budget constraints. This change was eventually scuttled by a protest by supporters of a popular monk that had raised almost US$14 million to bolster the country's currency reserves (Satitniramai 2007).

Attempts were also made to restructure the corporate finance regulatory structure in the aftermath of the crisis. In banking, this meant stricter requirements on the role of directors and lending practices (Pathan et al. 2008; Kubo 2006). As will be seen in the next period, these reforms also had little effect.

Sectoral Policy: Sectoral policy was highly particularistic in this period. In 1997, PM Chuan drew up a Master Plan for Public Sector Reform, which sought to streamline, professionalize, and clean up the policy-making and implementation process, focusing on outputs and outcomes (Punyaratabandhu and Unger 2009). The program was far-reaching and continued throughout Chuan's term in office but was beset by continual assault from factions and coalition partners in the cabinet (*The Nation (Thailand)* 2000). Despite PM Chuan's reputation as a clean politician, the incentives created by the EVP government ensured that, as with the period immediately prior to the crisis, corruption was rampant. The price of forming a government and remaining in power was that the Democrat party would have to ensure that its coalition partners had enough lucrative cabinet postings to fuel electoral machines in their home constituencies (Straits Times 1999; Tang 1998).

This process also undermined the Industrial Restructuring Plan designed by respected technocrat Sompop Amatayakul to facilitate greater coordination and competitiveness (Doner 2009). Early on the cabinet fought for greater control of the program, ostensibly to "ensure that its industrial restructuring is in line with plans by other agencies" (*Bangkok Post* 1998). The members of the FTI expressed skepticism, asking "whether all the changes [to the laws] could be made in such a relatively short time" (*Bangkok Post* 1998). Government delays and infighting ultimately led to a situation where the loans provided to business were both slower and more expensive than market-based loans (*The Nation (Thailand)* 1999; Thongrung 2000). The program ultimately failed to lead to significant restructuring (*Bangkok Post* 2000).

3.5.3 Economic Governance Institutions

Corporate Governance Institutions: The East Asian economic crisis massively transformed the financial landscape in Thailand. Major financial institutions that had large debt exposure in foreign currencies were crippled by the 1997 devaluation while firms with low debt coming into the crisis were in a good position to buy out failing companies in the resulting 'fire sale'. The value of the stock market plummeted and remained low throughout the period.

The formal rules and laws that are meant to facilitate liberal corporate governance were strengthened as reforms were pushed through in the wake of the crisis. New bankruptcy laws were implemented and courts established, organizations were created to work-out debt and non-performing loans, and new regulatory requirements were written compelling firms to strengthen audit committees and appoint external directors. But these formal reforms had little actual impact on business practices and family firms (new and old) and rapidly reestablished themselves as the dominant form of firm organization (White 2004).

The five major commercial banks suffered tremendous initial losses. Only Siam Commercial Bank, aided by the Crown Property Bureau's deep pockets and political power, and the Bank of Ayutthaya managed to stave off a loss of family control (Table 3.9).

As with firm corporate governance, the laws and regulations governing bank practices underwent significant reform after the crisis. Foreign investors were allowed to own 100% of banks, the BoT established 'Fit and Proper' criteria for board members of banks including limiting the number of boards on which they can serve and requiring experience, prohibitions on lending to connected parties (such as directors) were put in place, and banks were required to report non-performing loans regularly. These reforms, coupled with the changes in ownership structure seem to have had an impact on the behavior of the large banks, though they remained removed from international standards (Polsiri and Wiwattanakantang 2006).

Though the distribution of wealth among Thailand's most powerful families was shifted significantly in this period, family conglomerates remained the primary vehicle for corporate governance.

> More than five years after the crisis, and 2–4 years after these reforms were introduced, listed companies are still run by majority shareholders more like closely-held and opaque family businesses than transparent, professional or rule-based—e.g., "modern"—firms. New or enhanced regulations and formal institutions—such as bankruptcy laws and courts, debt and non- performing loan work-out organizations, audit committees, external directors, regulatory agencies—have not proven effective as monitoring and sanctioning mechanisms promoting better corporate governance practices as defined by Western observers…In essence, the wide range of corporate governance reforms has had essentially no impact on the management and behavior of Thai fims, private or listed. (White 2004)

Table 3.9 Thai commercial banks before and after the asian crisis in 1997

Commercial bank (before crisis)	*Largest shareholder (before crisis)*	*Resolution on or after 1997 crisis*	*Commercial bank (after crisis)*	*Largest shareholder (after crisis)*
Bangkok Bank	Sophonpanich	Recapitalized by foreign sale	Bangkok Bank	HSBC Banks (UK)
Krung Thai Bank	Government	Recapitalized by the government	Krung Thai Bank	Government
Thai Farmers Bank	Lamsam family	Recapitalized	Kasikorn Bank	State street and Trust Company (US)
Siam Commercial Bank	The Crown Property Bureau	Recapitalized	Siam Commercial Bank	The Crown Property Bureau
Siam City Bank	Srifuengfung and Mahadamrongkul	Recapitalized in 1998 and in 2000	Siam City Bank	Government
Bank of Ayudhya	Ratanarak family	Recapitalized	Bank of Ayudhya	Ratanarak family
Bank of Asia	Phatraprasith family	Recapitalized by foreign sale to a Dutch strategic partner in 1998	Bank of Asia	ABN-Amro Bank (Dutch)
Nakornthon Bank	Wang Lee family	Nationalized and subsequently privatized in 1998 by foreign sale to a UK strategic partner, Standard Chartered Bank	Standard Chartered Nakornthon Bank	Standard Chartered Bank (UK)
Thai Danu Bank	Tuchinda and Rassanon families	Recapitalized by foreign sale to Development Bank of Singapore (DBS) in 2000	DBS Thai Danu Bank	DBS (Singapore)
Thai Military Bank	Thai Defense Forces	Recapitalized	Thai Military Bank	Government
Union Bank of Bangkok	Cholvijam family	Intervened and recapitalized by integration with Krung Thai Thanakit Finance to form Bank Thai in 1998	Bank Thai	Government

(*Continued*)

Table 3.9 (Continued)

Commercial bank (before crisis)	*Largest shareholder (before crisis)*	*Resolution on or after 1997 crisis*	*Commercial bank (after crisis)*	*Largest shareholder (after crisis)*
Bangkok Metropolitan Bank	Techapaibul and Siriwattanapakdee families	Intervened in 1998 and merged with Siam City Bank in 2002	N/A	N/A
First Bangkok City Bank	Siriwattanapakdee family	Intervened, recapitalized and integrated with state owned Krung Thai Bank in 1998	N/A	N/A
Bangkok Bank of Commerce	Tantipipatpong fam-ily	Intervened and closed down in 1998 by transferring its best assets to KTB	N/A	N/A
Laem thong Bank	Chansrichawala fam-ily	Intervened and integrated with new state owned Radanasin Bank in 1998. Later in 2000, Radansin Bank recapitalized again by foreign sale to United Overseas Bank of Singapore (UOB)	UOB Radanasin Bank	United Overseas Bank (Singapore)
NA	NA	Thanachart bank commenced its operation as on 2001	Thanachart Bank	Government

Source (Pathan et al. 2008)

Vongvipanond and Wichitaksorn investigate the impact that the crisis had upon ownership and control patterns in Thai firms (Vongvipanond and Wichitaksorn 2005). They found, for their sample of firms facing distress, changes in ownership to be less substantial and widespread than in US firms facing similar financial distresses. Table 3.10 details their findings. Most family firms that lost some degree of ownership still retained effective control (i.e., retained at least a 20% share). The average holdings of the controlling shareholder in the sample went from 65% in 1996 to 24% in 2005.

Table 3.10 Change in ownership and control after the crisis

Level of	*Number of firms*	*Percent of total*	*Number of firms*	*Percent of firms*
Change	(Ownership change)	(Ownership change)	(Control change)	(Control change)
Less than 25%	32	46	3	17
25–50%	8	12	0	0
50–75%	11	16	4	22
More than 75%	18	26	11	61
Total	69	100	18	100

Source (Vongvipanond and Wichitaksorn 2005) Changes from pre-1996 to 2005

3.5.4 Electrical/Electronic Industry

As with the rest of the economy, the major firms in the electronics industry underwent substantial changes in the years following the crisis. The changes in ownership requirements coupled with the massively devalued baht encouraged foreign JV partners to buy out their local partners.

The government's 'Product Champions' effort to create a one-stop center for exporters specifically targeted electrical and electronics products (*Bangkok Post* 1998). The government's Industrial Restructuring Plan also targeted electronics and electricals but, as noted earlier, failed to spur effective coordination and upgrading because of the particularistic demands of coalition partners. In early 1999, the government approved the Electronics Master Plan which sought to coordinate policy by pursuing the following goals:

> 1) To create world class quality systems of support and production consisting of: -Systems to buy, sell and exchange parts and components within the industry - Creation of the Electrical and Electronics Institute - Restructuring of the entire import tax system. 2) To increase the value-added processes of the Thai portion of assembly and production, including: -Concentration on the highest volume export products - Support integration of the entire value chain for small and medium sized enterprises - To increase full cycle productivity. 3) To promote and create Thai brand names. 4) To improve the skills of both Thai management and labor. (Brenden 1999)

The EEIC opposed the plan to create the Electrical and Electronics Institute because secretary-general Saengchai Ekapatanapanich thought the government ought to use the existing National Electronics Institute rather than make a new one. With an eye toward the possibility of even more fragmentation, he argued that "If the centre cannot perform its role as a one-stop centre, it should concentrate on coordinating the work of different government agencies" (*Bangkok Post* 1998).

The two firms with coordinative corporate shareholding structures established in the semidemocratic period underwent major changes. Kulthorn Kirby fared well early on in the crisis but a large exposure to foreign-denominated loans hurt the group as the Baht faltered. Trading was suspended as shareholder equity became negative. The firm successfully restructured its debts by converting loans into equity and issuing new shares and selling holdings in subsidiaries.[12] Trade was permitted to resume in 2000 (*Bangkok Post* 2000). The Simakulthorn family actually increased its control of the company as a result of the crisis, increasing its share from 56.55% in 1996 to 72.54% in 2005 (Vongvipanond and Wichitaksorn 2005).

Thai CRT was also hit early on in the crisis but attempted to make a shift from television tubes to computer monitor tubes with the formation of CRT Display Technology in mid-1998 (Changsorn 1998). Though it had large foreign loans, its debt-to-equity ratio was moderate. Even though Siam Cement, the Thai anchor of Thai CRT, decided to sell its stake in the company in late 1999, it continued to improve and expand operations. CRT Display Technology, the Thai CRT subsidiary, joined with Sony to produce 17-inch computer monitors in 2000 (Changsorn 2000). SCG was still looking for buyers of Thai CRT when it purchased Mitsubishi's stake in the company in early 2001.

The large JV firms also underwent important changes, but most remained family controlled. Sanyo Universal Electronics (SUE) accrued massive losses following the economic crisis, with negative net worth for two fiscal years. It delisted from the stock exchange in 2001 as it tried to streamline and restructure its operations (Asia Pulse 2001; Thai News Service 2001). National Thai, Matushita Electric's JV in Thailand spun off several departments in 1998 and increased investment in Televisions and audio equipment production for export (Newswire 1998). Mitsubishi's Kang Yong Electric also suffered, but less severely.

After the crisis hit, the Federation of Thai Industries attempted to reassert itself as something more than a lobbying vehicle. Its 1997 internal election was the first to be hotly contested. It began a more forward-looking program for Thai industry, including a plan to foster the development of industrial clusters, completed in February of 2001 (*The Nation (Thailand)* 2001). Attempts to start a new wafer fabrication plant in the IC industry, both public and private, failed to gain steam (*Bangkok Post* 2000).

3.6 Single Party Rule (2001–2006)

3.6.1 Constraints

The first election of the new constitution produced an unprecedented concentration of political power in the parliament. Thaksin Shinawatra, an enormously wealthy multimedia mogul formed the Thai Rak Thai (TRT) party on a platform that was both populist and pro-business. TRT won 248 of the 500 seats in the lower chamber and formed a coalition government. In the following years, TRT joined with and swallowed many of the smaller parties, leaving only the Democrat and Chart Thai parties as a visible opposition (Phongpaichit and Baker 2004).

Veto Players: The reforms that came into effect for the 2001 elections led to a substantial reduction in the number of veto players for two main reasons. First, as intended by the constitutional reformers, the change to a mixed single-member-district and party-list electoral system reduced the number of political parties that won seats and produced smaller-sized coalitions (Lijphart 1999; Hicken 2002, 2006, 2007; Phongpaichit and Baker 2004). The two main parties were TRT and the Democrat Party with a few smaller parties fighting to remain relevant. TRT came out of the election with just 3 seats short of the 251 needed for a clear majority. It formed a coalition government with Chart Thai and the New Aspiration Parties. TRT's already strong position vis-à-vis its coalition partners was substantially strengthened in early 2002 when the New Aspiration Party was absorbed by TRT, giving it a healthy majority of 296 seats.

Second, party factions lost considerable influence under the new constitution. The incentives created by the new electoral system meant increases in both the power of party leadership and the value of party labels. Party leaders, with their newfound ability to choose the ranking of party list candidates, had greater power to reward loyal party members and punish those that threatened to withdraw from the party. The end of the multi-member districts also reduced the benefits of intra-party competition and increased the value of party labels. Additionally, the mandated 90-day waiting period after a candidate left one party before he could join another, together with the ability of the PM to call snap elections, successfully bound the factions to the highly centralized TRT. Without the threat of party-switching, faction leaders lost considerable leverage (Hicken 2007; Phongpaichit and Baker 2004). Thus, though many of the factions that had led to the instability of the coalition government and post-crisis periods still existed under Thai Rak Thai's banner, their power was dramatically diminished. As such, I do not count the party factions as veto players in the single-party period.

Over time, the popularity of TRT's populist policies further undermined the pork-fueled electoral machines of the faction leaders. Rural voters increasingly voted for the party platform over the individual candidates (Phongpaichit and Baker 2004). In its first year, TRT was dependent on at least one of its coalition partners for its majority. From 2002 on, it completely dominated every policy arena, including macro and micro economic policies. With a majority of seats and a centrally controlled party, Thaksin's TRT operated as the sole veto player in the TRT period. The party, as directed by Thaksin, had direct control of macro and sectoral economic policies.

Systemic Vulnerability: External threats continued to be limited during this period. In southern Thailand, an ongoing low-level conflict with an indigenous Muslim separatist movement grew to a full insurgency (Croissant 2005; Hefner 2002). Scores of domestic Islamic groups with varying objectives, international connections, and methods struggled with the government. Though the violence was intense, its limited geographic scope meant that there was little fear that the continued existence of the state was endangered.

State resources were still stretched thin when Thai Rak Thai came to power. By 2003, however, TRT had turned budget deficits into surpluses. The populist-business coalition of the TRT regime was broad based and the government was committed to keeping the masses appeased. Before the 2001 election, TRT reached out to farmer groups and others that were dissatisfied with the Democrat party's IMF-directed brand of neoliberalism. The election platform included a number of policies designed to appeal to the majority in the provinces, including a debt moratorium, a low-cost health care program, and a village fund. Though, once in office, Thaksin proved willing to use coercion, manipulation, and force to limit mass protest, he delivered on promised policies and actively sought to maintain popular support (Phongpaichit and Baker 2004).

With low external threat, moderate but declining resource scarcity, and a broad coalition, Thailand had moderate levels of vulnerability during this period. The systemic vulnerability argument suggests that the policy environment should be moderately particularistic.

3.6.2 Policy Environment

Macroeconomic Policy: The macroeconomic policy environment was only moderately predictable in the single-party era and was sometimes used to achieve particularistic ends. Running on a platform that contained both economic-nationalist and progressive elements, Thai Rak Thai sought to achieve its ends by expanding GDP and stimulating the domestic market as quickly as possible. All elements of macro policy were brought to bear to achieve these policy goals. Though these goals remained paramount, the policy means used by TRT to achieve them were experimental and subject to trial and error (based on both economic and political merits).

Still reeling from the East Asian economic crisis, Thaksin continued the Democrat party's Keynesian fiscal stimulus policy, but was limited by already high levels of public debt (Baker and Phongpaichit 2014). The official budget was augmented by a variety of semi-public financing schemes designed both to enhance the stimulus' multiplier effect and reward rural supporters. In the 2002–2003 period these loans were estimated to be 10–17% of the size of the official budget (Sussangkarn and Vichyanond 2007; Baker and Phongpaichit 2005). The majority of these quasi-fiscal financing schemes were made up of relatively small loans for SMEs and rural families, groups with low rates of default that had been largely neglected by the large commercial banks. This was part of a larger plan to restructure the financial sector:

> In January 2004, the Thai government announced the Financial Sector Master Plan, which signaled the banking industry's return to normal from a post-crisis mode. The visions of the plan are threefold: (1) to broaden general access to financial services, especially for rural and low-income households; (2) to increase efficiency of the financial sector; and (3) to protect consumers by promoting information disclosure of financial institutions and introducing a deposit insurance. The substantial part of the plan addresses measures to increase efficiency of the financial sector

> through enhancing market mechanism. These include:(i) relaxing entry to the banking sector by promoting upgrade of finance or credit financier companies to commercial banks; (ii) relaxing regulations on opening branches in dense areas; and (III) relaxing restrictions on foreign financial institutions' scope of business and opening branches. (Kubo 2006, 326)

Portions of several state-owned enterprises were sold off as a way to raise revenue and limit drains on state revenues without blatantly betraying his strong public stand against the IMF's privatization plans. These sizable stakes in the 'corporatized' enterprises, including the massive government petroleum corporation PTT, were sold quickly and cheaply, and found their way into the hands of political supporters and industrial allies (Baker and Phongpaichit 2014; Phongpaichit and Baker 2004). Such moves, unlike the semi-public financing scheme were narrowly targeted.

PM Thaksin's record on monetary policy was mixed. He pressured the BoT to raise interest rates in early 2001 and replaced the governor when he refused (Sussangkarn and Vichyanond 2007). But during a similar conflict in 2004, he sided with the BoT over his Finance Minister (Sussangkarn and Vichyanond 2007). Thaksin's administration, despite having an economically nationalistic platform, pursued an open trade policy. They created bilateral free trade agreements with many important trading partners and was pursuing more with Japan, the United States, and several other countries.

Sectoral Policy: The sectoral policy environment remained particularistic throughout the single party period. The most flagrant instances of particularistic policies occurred where Thaksin's own industrial concerns were at issue. Thaksin's telecommunications empire, which had been built by means of lucrative government concessions in the coalition government and post crisis periods, flourished once Thaksin gained control of the policy-making apparatus (Phongpaichit and Baker 2004). Thaksin's supporters, allies, and friends likewise prospered, while his enemies withered. The concentration of power meant that harnessing and maintaining access channels was more critical than ever.

The results of an investigation into the economic benefits of political office for family conglomerates demonstrates the continued role of particularism in sectoral policy. The study found that during the single-party era politically connected firms were able to channel government support to their conglomerates, leading to extraordinary gains in market valuation and market share (Bunkanwanicha and Wiwattanakantang 2008).

3.6.3 *Economic Governance Institutions*

With a moderately particularistic macroeconomic policy environment and a highly particularistic sectoral policy environment, this framework predicts hierarchical economic governance institutions.

Corporate Governance Institutions: Corporate governance institutions were hierarchical in the single-party period. The stock market remained an important vehicle for firms to raise money but ownership and control continued to be tightly bound. Commercial banks, still reeling from the crisis, continued to focus on large customers at the expense of consumers and SMEs. "The Thai financial sector focused its services on the advanced sectors, with little attention paid to the less privileged groups. For example, roughly 23% of small- and medium-sized enterprises (SME) lacked access to credit from the financial system, and so did 58% of the people who had low income (below $US5000 per annum). They could only get credit if they had adequate and reliable guarantee or collateral. These underserved groups had to resort to informal sources of funds as well as cooperatives" (Sussangkarn and Vichyanond 2007, 111–112). Thaksin's efforts to expand credit to finance small-scale borrowers and SMEs were resisted by the banks (Phongpaichit and Baker 2004).

Despite the structural changes in the financial industry that occurred in the wake of the crisis, the commercial banking sector remained highly oligopolistic (Kubo 2006; Nakornthab 2007). New family empires emerged to join the families that survived the crash, leaving family conglomerates as the dominant form of corporate governance. Table 3.9 shows the predominance of concentrated ownership in a sample of 384 listed firms in 2006. By 2006 just over half of listed firms were controlled by families, higher than before the crisis (Phongpaichit and Baker 2008, 44) (Table 3.11).

Table 3.11 Percentage of shares held by top ten shareholders

	Number of firms	*Percent*
More than 80%	105	27.3
61–80%	185	48.2
41–60%	70	18.2
21–40%	20	5.2
Less than 20%	4	1
Total	384	100

Source (Phongpaichit and Baker 2008)

Inter-firm Linkage Institutions: In 2002 Thaksin began meeting directly with the heads of the FTI to vet industry concerns (Wiriyapong 2002c). Unlike Prem's JPPCC this program was highly centralized and government-directed. Still, the consultations provided important programmatic input by industry and led to concrete action, including the championing of the Federation's cluster plan, support for SMEs, and improving infrastructure (Wiriyapong 2002a).

3.6.4 Electrical/Electronic Industry

Kulthorn Kirby (KK) emerged from the crisis in a healthy position and continued to strengthen its position in the A/C and refrigeration industries. The compressor manufacturer acquired a majority stake in Chachoengsao Casting Works from Sanyo in 2004 and subsequently purchased the Sanyo's compressor producing assets. The move doubled KK's production capacity from 400,000 to 800,000 units a year (Thai News Service 2004b; Knight Ridder Tribune Business News 2004). In 2005, the company had a 40% share in the local A/C compressor market and an 80% in the local refrigerator compressor market (Thai News Service 2005).

In 2002, Sanyo closed refrigerator plants in Japan and relocated them to Thailand. Sanyo bought out its Thai JV partners' stake in SUE in 2004 and subsequently invested 2 billion Baht in expanding refrigerators, freezers, and washing machines, simultaneously closing white-goods plants in Singapore (Nikkei Report 2004; *The Nation (Thailand)* 2004).

In 2002, the FTI criticized the lack of a clear government strategy with regard to the sector (Wiriyapong 2002b). Two years later the Electrical and Electronics and Allied Industry Club of the sought collectively to create a Thai brand in the home appliance industry. Spearheaded by FTI president Suraporn Simakulthorn, of Kulthorn Kirby, the company would manufacture and export refrigerators, washing machines, and air conditioners (Thai News Service 2004c). Despite the potential objections of foreign partners, many of the families in the electrical and electronics industries pursued the project. The EEAIC proposed the plan, which would include the MoF, the Electricity Generating Authority of Thailand and the Metropolitan Electricity Authority as partners, to the Ministry of Industry (Thai News Service 2004a). It moved gradually forward but did not reach fruition before Mr. Thaksin was forced out of office.

3.7 Conclusion

Between 1957 and 2006, Thailand experienced six different configurations of veto players and degrees of vulnerability. Table 14 highlights the findings for each period. In the military rule period, a single veto player government facing moderate vulnerability was expected to limit the degree of particularism in the economy in order to combat the vulnerability. The period played out as expected, with the government employing technocrats to ensure broadly targeted policy goals but using sectoral policy for personal enrichment and to maintain political support.

The instability period featured a high degree of regime instability. As such the framework predicts a highly particularistic policy environment. As expected, the instability led to an unstable, policy narrowly targeted policy environment. Moderate vulnerability and a mixed single and EVP government in the semi-democracy period was expected to result in a policy environment with limited particularism. The observed environment was again a mix of broadly targeted macroeconomic policy and a sectoral policy that was limited in scope but narrowly targeted to benefit elected politicians. A combination of low vulnerability and an EVP government in the coalition period was expected to produce a highly particularistic policy environment. Whether governed by clearly pork-fueled governments or ostensibly reform-oriented, the policy environment in this period was narrowly targeted as ministries ruled by different parties sought to maximize their own gains.

The increased vulnerability caused by the economic crisis was not expected to bring about a decline in the level of particularism. As expected, the EVP government, despite promises, could not overcome the tendency toward policy balkanization. The moderate vulnerability in the beginning of the single party rule period was expected to constrain the degree of particularism. But declining vulnerability throughout the period would lessen those constraints. As expected, the Thaksin government pursued a number of broadly targeted policies in the start of his term but over time these gave way to narrowly targeted programs (Table 3.12).

With the policy environment matching expectations, I will now consider their impact on the economic governance institutions.

In the military rule period, the moderately particularistic policy environment was expected to produce a mix of hierarchical and coordinative economic governance structures. The overall economy was dominated by

Table 3.12 Constraints, policy environment, and economic governance institutions in Thailand

Period	*Constraints*	*Policy environment*	*Corporate governance (overall economy)*	*Corporate governance (electronics/electrical)*	*Interfirm linkages (overall economy)*	*Interfirm linkages (electronics/ electrical)*
Military rule	• Single Veto Player • Moderate Vulnerability	• Moderately particularistic policy environment	• Dominance of family banks and diversified family business conglomerates	• Family firms partner with Japanese producers. Mix of diversified conglomerates and specialized firms	• Mostly weak coordination	• No strong coordinating institutions
Instability	• Regime instability • High vulnerability	• Highly particularistic policy environment	• Dominance of family banks and diversified family business conglomerates	• Primarily family firms partnered with foreign producers. Mix of diversified conglomerates and specialized firms	• No strong coordinating institutions	• No strong coordinating institutions • EEAIC created in the association of thai industries at the end of this period
Semi-democracy	• Single veto player (macro) • Excessive veto players (sectoral) • Moderate vulnerability	• Particularism limited to sectoral policy	• Dominance of family banks and diversified family business conglomerates. • Increased use of capital markets for finance of family firms	• Continued dominance of family firms partnered with foreign producers. Mix of diversified conglomerates and specialized firms• New entrants with coordinative governance	• Rapid expansion of business associations, more intensive coordination and direct public–private consultation	• ACRC and the FTI work to develop upstream compressor capabilities • EEAIC and the FTI work to develop upstream CRT capabilities

(*Continued*)

Table 3.12 (Continued)

Period	*Constraints*	*Policy environment*	*Corporate governance (overall economy)*	*Corporate governance (electronics/electrical)*	*Interfirm linkages (overall economy)*	*Interfirm linkages (electronics/ electrical)*
Coalitional governments	• Excessive veto players. • Low vulnerability	• Highly particularistic policy environment	• Dominance of family banks and diversified family business conglomerates • Increased use of capital markets for finance of family firms.	• Continued dominance of family firms partnered with foreign producers. Mix of diversified conglomerates and specialized firms• Coordinative governance structures remain	• Some lobbying. No strong coordinating activities	• Limited lobbying on tariff issues. No new coordinating activities
Post-crisis	• Excessive veto players • Moderate vulnerability.	• Highly particularistic policy environment	• Radical changes in ownership but diversified family firms remain dominant	• Similar to overall economy and foreign partners increase their shares• Firms with coordinative governance structure become family controlled	• Failed attempts to strengthen coordination	• FTI and EEAIC call for development of Thai brands at the end of this period
Single party rule	• Single veto player • Moderate & decreasing vulnerability.	• Increasingly particularistic policy environment	• Family firms and banks remain the dominant form of governance	• Family firms and banks remain the dominant form of governance	• Attempts at public–private consultation • Several cluster initiatives started	• FTI and EEAIC work to establish Thai appliance brand but project remains unfinished

family-controlled banks and diversified, family-controlled conglomerates. The electronics and electricals sector was largely dominated by family firms but they were a mix of diversified business groups and firms specialized in the EEI sector. There was less coordinative corporate governance than expected in this period. Inter-firm linkage institutions were, aside from some coordination in the rice industry, generally hierarchical in this period, with weak coordination along familial/ethnic lines despite government efforts to foster the development of stronger business associations.

The instability period featured a highly particularistic policy environment and was expected to result in hierarchical corporate governance institutions. The family controlled firms of the earlier period remained and the major new entrant in the sector was also owned a diversified family business group. Inter-firm linkage institutions remained hierarchical.

Particularism was constrained in the semi-democratic period and the policy environment was expected to produce a mix of hierarchical and coordinative corporate governance institutions. Family firms remained dominant but two important new firms were created with a corporate governance structure that included many competing firms. Business associations and public–private associations flourished in this period and increased the scope of cooperation.

The policy environment in the coalitional government period was highly particularistic. This was expected to result in the dominance of hierarchical corporate governance institutions. The family groups of earlier periods continued to flourish, as did the coordinative firms of the semi-democratic period. With the influx of foreign capital channeled through family-controlled banks, new hierarchically structured emerged. Coordination in inter-firm linkage institutions declined in this period.

Despite promises of reform, particularism remained high in the post-crisis policy environment. The economic turmoil caused great changes in ownership patterns but family business groups remained dominant. The coordinative firms of the semi-democratic period lost their downstream shareholders. Inter-firm linkage institutions remained hierarchically oriented in this period.

The period of single party rule had moderate but increasing particularism and was expected to produce a mix of coordinative institutions. Family business groups remained dominant in the economy. Inter-firm linkage institutions attempted greater coordination in this period but were unsuccessful. In the EEI sector there was an effort to create a Thai brand of appliance under joint ownership of Thai manufacturers, but it did not come to fruition.

Thus, the framework provides a compelling explanation of the link between political constraints, the policy environment and the economic governance institutions that developed in Thailand since the 1960s. The next chapter evaluates the ability of the framework to explain the emergence of economic governance in Malaysia.

Notes

1. The policy conflicts that arose between Dr. Puey and Sarit will be addressed in the next section as they cannot be used as evidence of whether Dr. Puey had any actual institutionally guaranteed veto power. Though Dr. Puey's technical expertise as Thailand's premier economist was extremely useful to Sarit, he ultimately served at Sarit's pleasure. Though the Sarit and Thanom regimes depended on economic development to provide long-term legitimacy to their regimes, it is extremely unlikely that their political position would have been immediately affected by the removal of Dr. Puey. There may have been real costs in terms of business confidence by such action but its impact on the ability of Sarit/Thanom to maintain the support of the military would have been minimal.
2. Thitinan discusses the relationship between Sarit and Puey at length (Pongsudhirak 2002).
3. The large Thai banks, many of which grew out of the rice industry, did have some success in coordinating in that industry. For more on this see Christensen (1993).
4. Early in the semi-democratic period there was conflict between Prem and his deputy PM Boonchu over spending. Boonchu's desire to engage in 'pump-priming' ran contrary to the austerity program preferred by Prem. The conflict, which ended in the dismissal of Boonchu and the temporary withdrawal of his Social Action Party from the ruling coalition, demonstrated Prem's sole authority over fiscal policy (Laothamatas 1992).
5. For more on the multi-member multi-vote system and its effect on the party system, see (Hicken 2002, 2007).
6. Though a 1979 amendment to the Commercial Banking Act of 1962 restricting individual holdings was enacted, banking families were able to circumvent its limits.
7. Because the Anand governments were so brief, they are not considered in detail.

8. The brief Anand I and II governments were periods of uncertainty and are excluded from this analysis.
9. This excludes the 1991 Investment Promotion Act created under the appointed Anand government.
10. They will be described in greater detail in the inter-firm linkage section of this period.
11. The implications of this will be discussed in greater detail in the conclusion.
12. Samarn Sudto and Suphaphan Plengmaneepun, "Kulthorn Kirby - Exports Seen as Saviour After Firm's Historic Loss," *Bangkok Post*, 1998; Reuters News, "Thai Stock Exchange Suspends Trade in 15 Firms," 1999; Oranan Paweewun, "KK Restructures Bt2.2bn Debts," *The Nation (Thailand)*, 1999; Bangkok Post, "Debt Restructuring: Kulthorn Kirby Plan Accepted," December 1999; *Bangkok Post*, "Three Firms Say They're Ready to Restructure," 1999.

References

Absence of State Commitments and Political Instability Remain Major Hurdles. (2000, October 12). *Bangkok Post.*

Amonvadekul, P. (1989). *Changes in international competitiveness a case study of the electrical machinery industry in Thailand, 1975–1985.* Bangkok: Thammasat University.

Anuchitworawong, C. (2007). Credit access and poverty reduction. *TDRI Quarterly Review, 22(4).*

Asia Pulse. (2001). Japan's Sanyo Thai joint venture falls into negative net worth.

Backman, M. (1999). *Asian eclipse: Exposing the dark side of business in Asia.* Hoboken: Wiley.

Baker, C., & Phongpaichit, P. (2005). *A history of Thailand.* Melbourne: Cambridge University Press.

Baker, C., & Phongpaichit, P. (2014). *A history of Thailand.* Melbourne: Cambridge University Press.

Bankers Applaud Choice of Minister. (1990, August 28). *Bangkok Post.*

Bangkok Post. (1998). Economic Policy.

Brenden, C. (1999). Electronic components market. *Industry Sector Analysis (Chamber World Network).*

Bunkanwanicha, P., & Wiwattanakantang, Y. (2008). Allocating risk across pyramidal tiers: Evidence from Thai business groups. *CEI Working Paper Series.*

Centre Wrestles with Bureaucracy. (1998, November 12). *Bangkok Post.*

Changsorn, P. (1998). Thai $136m computer display plant on track. *The Nation.*

Changsorn, P. (2000). Local Firm, Sony Plan Joint Line. *The Nation.*

Cheesman, B. (1998). Corporate Thailand seeks new influence with leadership poll. *Business Times (Singapore)*.

Chaiyasoot, N. (1987). *Commercial banking in Thailand*. Canberra: Australian National University.

Chip Project In Thailand. (1994, December 30). *New York Times*.

Christensen, S. (1993). *Coalitions and collective choice: The politics of institutional change in Thai agriculture*. Madison: The University of Wisconsin.

Claessens, S., Djankov, S., & Lang, L. H. P. (2000). The separation of ownership and control in East Asian corporations. *Journal of Financial Economics, 58*(1–2), 81–112.

Claessens, S., & Fan, J. P. H. (2002). Corporate governance in Asia: A survey. *International Review of Finance, 3*(2), 71–103.

Cluster Plan for Industry Finalized. (2001, February 16). *The Nation (Thailand)*.

Compressor Firm to Boost Capital. (1990, July 2). *Bangkok Post*.

Croissant, A. (2005). Unrest in South Thailand: Contours, causes, and consequences since 2001. *Contemporary Southeast Asia, 27*(1), 21–44.

Doner, R. F. (2009). *The politics of uneven development: Thailand's economic growth in comparative perspective*. New York: Cambridge University Press. http://doi.org/10.1080/00472336.2011.553054.

Doner, R. F., & Laothamatas, A. (1994). Thailand: economic and political gradualism. In S. Haggard & S. B. Webb (Eds.), *Voting for reform: Democracy, political liberalization, and economic adjustment* (Vol. 94). A World Bank Publication.

Fagan, P., Foley, F., & Gilson, S. (2001). Alphatec Electronics PCL 107. In S. Claessens, S. Djankov, & A. Mody (Eds.), *Resolution of financial distress: an international perspective on the design of bankruptcy laws*. World Bank Institute.

Far Eastern Economic Review. (1998). Thailand: Politics as usual: Corruption resurfaces under pro-reform government.

Felker, G. (1998). Malaysia's industrial technology development: Firms, policies, and political economy. *Industrial technology development in Malaysia: Industry and firm studies*. New York: Routledge.

Felker, G. (1999). Malaysia in 1998: A cornered tiger bares its claws. *Asian Survey, 39*(1), 43–54.

Fletcher, R. (2001). A holistic approach to internationalisation. *International Business Review, 10*(1), 25–49.

Fletcher, R., & Barrett, N. (2001). Embeddedness and the evolution of global networks: An Australian case study. *Industrial Marketing Management, 30*(7), 561–573.

Financial Times. (1996). Talking Softly and Carrying a Big Chip.

Freezing out Some Locals. (1977, June 18). *The Economist*.

Government Reforms Need Careful Thinking. (2000, August 7). *The Nation (Thailand)*.

Govt Agencies Seen as Major Achievements. (1989, December 27). *Bangkok Post*.

Govt Urged to Release Funds. (1999, January 12). *The Nation (Thailand)*.

Hatch, W., & Yamamura, K. (1996). *Asia in japan's embrace: Building a regional production alliance*. Cambridge: Cambridge University Press.

Hefner, R. W. (2002). Islam and Asian Security. *Strategic Asia*, 3.

Hewison, K. J. (1989). *Bankers and bureaucrats: Capital and the role of the state in Thailand. Monograph series / Yale University Southeast Asia Studies, Yale Center for International and Area Studies; 34.*

Hicken, A. (2002). *Parties, pork and policy: policymaking in developing democracies*. PhD dissertation, University of California San Diego.

Hicken, A. (2006). Party fabrication: Constitutional reform and the rise of Thai Rak Thai. *Journal of East Asian Studies*, *6*(3), 381–408.

Hicken, A. (2007). Omitted variables, intent, and counterfactuals: A response to Michael H. Nelson. *Journal of East Asian Studies*, *7*, 149–158.

Hirankasi, P. (2008). Foreign capital flows and stock market in developing countries: Some evidence from Thailand.

Jiji Press English News Service. (1987). BOI fails to decide on Thai–Japanese compressor venture.

Kamol Sukosol Electric Co. (2008). Company Background.

Khomate, M. (1997). *Industrial development: A case study of Thai television industry*. Bangkok: Thammasat University.

Knight Ridder Tribune Business News. (2004). Thai Compressor Manufacturer Plans Merger.

Krishnamurti, C., Ševic, A., & Ševic, Ž. (2005). Legal environment, firm-level corporate governance and expropriation of minority shareholders in Asia. *Economic Change and Restructuring*, *38*(1), 85–111.

Kubo, K. (2006). The degree of competition in the Thai banking industry before and after the East Asian crisis. *ASEAN Economic Bulletin*, *23*(3), 325.

Kulthorn Aims to be Top Compressor Maker. (1989, November). *Bangkok Post*, p. 20.

Kulthorn Group. (2009a). Kulthorn Kirby Foundry.

Kulthorn Group. (2009b). Thai Sintered Products Co.,Ltd.

Laothamatas, A. (1988). Business and politics in Thailand: New patterns of influence. *Asian Survey*, *28*(4), 451–470.

Laothamatas, A. (1992). *Business associations and the new political economy of Thailand: From bureaucratic polity to liberal corporatism*. Boulder: Westview Press.

Lauridsen, L. S. (2005). Foreign direct investment, linkage formation and supplier development in Thailand during the 1990s: The role of state governance. In R. Narula & S. Lall (Eds.), *Understanding FDI-assisted economic development* (p. 115). Oxfordshire: Routledge.

Lijphart, A. (1999). *Patterns of democracy: government forms and performance in thirty-six countries.* Yale University Press.

MacIntyre, A. (2003a). Institutions and investors: The politics of the economic crisis in Southeast Asia. *International Organization, 55*(1), 81–122.

MacIntyre, A. (2003b). *The power of institutions: Political architecture and governance.* Ithaca: Cornell University Press.

McVey, R. T. (2000). *Money and power in provincial Thailand.* Honolulu, HI: University of Hawaii Press.

Mitsubishi Affiliates to Meet Regional Suppliers. (1994). *Bangkok Post.*

Muscat, R. (1987). *Family Enterprise in Thailand.*

Muscat, R. (1990). *Thailand and The United States.* New York: Columbia University Press.

Muscat, R. (1994). *The fifth tiger: A study of Thai development policy.* Tokyo: United nations university press.

Nakornthab, D. (2007). Thai commercial banks one decade after the crisis: Assessment of risk to financial stability. Unpublished Manuscript, Bank of Thailand (July).

Narongchai, A. (1982). *Industrial restructuring in Thailand: The case of electronics and electrical industry.* The Industrial Management Co., Ltd.

Neher, C. D. (1988). Thailand in 1987: Semi-successful semi-democracy. *Asian Survey, 28*(2), 192–201.

Newswire, J. E. (1998). Matsushita to form AV manufacturing unit in Thailand.

Nikkei Report. (2004). Sanyo electric to revamp white goods production in SE Asia.

Niksch, L. A. (1989). Thailand in 1988: The economic surge. *Asian Survey, 29*(2), 165–173.

Opposition to Target Fiscal and Monetary Policy. (1990, December 27). *Bangkok Post.*

Pathan, S., Skully, M., & Wickramanayake, J. (2008). Reforms in Thai bank governance: The aftermath of the Asian financial crisis. *International Review of Financial Analysis, 17*(2), 345–362.

Phiphatseitham, K., & Yoshihara, K. (1983). *Business groups in Thailand.* Inst of Southeast Asian Studies.

Phongpaichit, P., & Baker, C. (1998). *Thailand's boom and bust.* Ching Mai: Silkworm Books.

Phongpaichit, P., & Baker, C. (2000). *Thailand's crisis.* Ching Mai: Silkworm Books.

Phongpaichit, P., & Baker, C. (2004). Thaksin: the business of politics in Thailand.

Phongpaichit, P., & Baker, C. (2008). *Thai Capital: After the 1997 crisis*. Iseas: Silkworm Books.

Polsiri, P., & Wiwattanakantang, Y. (2006). Corporate governance of banks in Thailand. *CEI Working Paper Series*.

Pongsudhirak, T. (2001). *Crisis from within: The politics of macroeconomic management in Thailand, 1947–1997*. London, UK: University of London.

Pongsudhirak, T. (2002). *Crisis from within: The politics of macroeconomic management in Thailand, 1947–1997*. London, UK: London School of Economics and Political Science (University of London).

Pramaul Softens His Stance on Bank Rate. (1989, December 18). *Bangkok Post*.

Priwan, Y. (1997). Moving to Next Stage too Costly, FTI Says. *Bangkok Post*.

Punyaratabandhu, S. (1998). Thailand in 1997: Financial crisis and constitutional reform. *Asian Survey, 38*(2), 161–167.

Punyaratabandhu, S. (1999). Thailand in 1998: A false sense of recovery. *Asian Survey, 39*(1), 80–88.

Punyaratabandhu, S., & Unger, D. H. (2009). Managing performance in a context of political clientelism: The case of Thailand. *The Many Faces of Public Management Reform in the Asia-Pacific* (p. 279). West Yorkshire: Emerald.

Restructuring—Industrial Plan too Unwieldy. (1998, June 1). *Bangkok Post*.

Restructuring SET to Ease Trading Criteria for 5 Banks. (2000, August 18). *Bangkok Post*.

Reuters News. (1998a). Democrats Say Thai Coalition Taking Shape.

Reuters News. (1998b). Neico buys 10 pct of Pensonic.

Reuters News. (1999). Thai Stock Exchange Suspends Trade in 15 Firms.

Ritchie, B. (2002). *Foreign direct investment and intellectual capital formation in Southeast Asia*. OECD Development Centre.

Ritchie, B. (2005). Progress through setback or mired in mediocrity? Crisis and institutional change in Southeast Asia. *Journal of East Asian Studies, 5*(2), 273–313.

Rock, M. T. (1994). Transitional democracies and the shift to export-led industrialization: Lessons from Thailand. *Studies in Comparative International Development (SCID), 29*(1), 18–37.

Satitniramai, A. (2007). *Weak state and political economy of Thailand: Ten years after the crisis*. *V.R.F.* (Vol. 434). Institute of Developing Economies, Japan External Trade Organization.

SCG Joint Ventures Reflect Export Campaign. (1989, August 10). *Bangkok Post*.

Siamwalla, A. (1997). Can a developing democracy manage its macroeconomy? The case of Thailand. *Thailand's boom and bust* (pp. 63–75). Ching Mai: Silkworm Books.

Siew-National Plans B700m Head Office. (1993, September 14). *Bangkok Post*.

Sirivedhin, T. (1998). Financial reform and the monetary transmission mechanism: the case of Thailand. *BIS Policy Papers*, 3.

Straits Times. (1999). Cabinet Reshuffle, but Chuan Retains Key Posts.

Suehiro, A. (1989). *Capital accumulation in Thailand, 1855–1985*. Centre for East Asian Cultural Studies.

Suehiro, A. (1993a). Capitalist development in postwar Thailand: Commercial bankers, industrial elite, and agribusiness groups. In R. T. McVey (Ed.), *Southeast Asian Capitalists* (pp. 35–63). Ithaca: Cornell University.

Suehiro, A. (1993b). Family business reassessed: Corporate structure and late-starting industrialization in Thailand. *Developing Economies, 31,* 378.

Suehiro, A. (2001). *Family business gone wrong? Ownership patterns and corporate performance in Thailand*. Asian Development Bank Institute.

Suehiro, A., & Wailerdsak, N. (2004). Family business in Thailand. *ASEAN Econimic Bulletin, 21*(1), 81–93.

Sussangkarn, C., & Vichyanond, P. (2007). Ten years after the financial crisis in Thailand: What has been learned or not learned? *Asian Economic Policy Review, 2*(1), 100.

Tang, E. (1998). Chuan Struggles to Keep Govt Intact. *Straits Times.*

Tanin Industrial. (1979, August). *ASSET International (Thai Language).*

Techakanont, K. (1997). An analysis of subcontracting system and technology transfer: A case study of the Thai television industry. *Unpublished Master thesis*, Faculty of Economics, Thammasat University, Bangkok, Thailand.

Thai CRT Produces First Local Television Tubes. (1989, September 22). *Bangkok Post.*

Thai News Service. (2001). Sanyo to delist from stock exchange Sanyo Universal Electric Plc (SUE) Informed the Stock Exchange.

Thai News Service. (2004a). FTI Wants Thai ELECTRIC APPLIANCES.

Thai News Service. (2004b). KKC Predicts Income of 4.5 Billion Baht this Year.

Thai News Service. (2004c). National Electrical Appliance Brand to be Established.

Thai News Service. (2005). Thailand Compressor Producer Kulthorn Group to Expand Production Facility.

The Investor. (1972). The electronics industry: Wide-open market for local producers.

Thongrung, W. (2000). Agencies Seek End to Industry Loan Scheme. *The Nation (Thailand).*

Tsebelis, G. (2002). *Veto players: How political institutions work*. Princeton: Princeton University Press.

Unger, D. (1998). *Building social capital in Thailand: Fibers, finance, and infrastructure*. New York: Cambridge Univ Press.

Vichit-Vadakan, J. (1985). Thailand in 1984: Year of administering rumors. *Asian Survey, 25*(2), 232–240.

Vongvipanond, P., & Wichitaksorn, N. (2005). Thailand corporate restructuring and pre-and post-crisis ownership and control. In *Paper presented at RIETI International Workshop* (Vol. Reform of).

White, S. (2004). Stakeholders, structure and the failure of corporate governance reform initiatives in post-crisis Thailand. *Asia Pacific Journal of Management, 21*(1), 103–122.

Zhang, X. (2010). The changing politics banking in Taiwan of and Central Thailand. *Crisis, 78*(3), 377–401.

Wiriyapong, N. (2002a). 5-point recovery strategy. *The Nation (Thailand)*.

Wiriyapong, N. (2002b). FTI Chief Puts Blame on Government. *The Nation (Thailand)*.

Wiriyapong, N. (2002c). Industrial development: Thaksin will lend an ear. *The Nation (Thailand)*.

Wong-Anan, N. (1994). Thai Legislators Take Their Tithe. *Asian Wall Street Journal*.

CHAPTER 4

Malaysia: Thriving Under Neglect

This chapter will compare the overall evolution of economic governance systems in the Federation of Malaysia with that of Penang, one of its most prosperous states. Due to a number of historical factors, Penang experienced structural and institutional circumstances that differed from the rest of the states in the Malaysian federation. Because these differences exist against a larger backdrop of geographic, developmental, and cultural similarities, we can observe whether veto players and vulnerability had the expected effects through the proposed mechanisms.

From independence until 1969, Malaysia's federal government was ruled by the Alliance, a block of closely-allied parties that represented the interests of elites from the country's three main ethnic groups: Malays, Chinese, and Indians. Though the United Malays National Organization (UMNO), which represented the majority Malay ethnic group, was dominant in the Alliance, the Malaysian Chinese Association (MCA) had sufficient influence to veto policies it found objectionable. *With a broad coalitional base, moderate external threats, and moderate but declining revenues from tin and rubber resources, the Alliance government was constrained from making radical policy shifts and providing narrowly targeted policies.*

Massive racial riots in 1969 brought substantial change to the Malaysian political structure. Malay leaders in UMNO sought to relive ethnic tensions by pursuing interventionist economic policies that sought to bring the rural Malay population out of poverty. With the threat of inter-ethnic violence, Chinese leaders in the MCA were much less willing to stand up to increasing UMNO-directed government encroachment into the

J.D. Moore, *Varieties of Capitalism in Southeast Asia*, The Political Economy of East Asia, DOI 10.1007/978-3-319-53700-9_4

economic sphere. This increased concentration of veto power together with higher government revenues from extractive resource reserves relaxed the constraints binding the federal government. It was thereafter freed to pursue policies that specifically targeted UMNO loyalists.

But a far different situation had emerged in the state of Penang. While the Alliance had ruled prior to the riots, the opposition Gerakan party won a majority in 1969. Despite merging with the Barisan Nasional (BN)—the Alliance's successor, in 1972, the party retained a high degree of autonomy and continued to compete directly with BN member MCA. As the only majority-Chinese state in the federation, Penang did not benefit from the Malay-directed largesse that the federal government was distributing. If it had been unable to keep ethnic tensions under control, the Penang state government would have had real reason to fear Federal domination. Penang's economic policy was thus decided by a one player government and faced high vulnerability.

Table 4.1 displays the divergence of structural and institutional factors in Malaysia and Penang.

The rest of the chapter will proceed as follows. First, I examine the overall relationships between structural and institutional factors, the policy environment, and governance institutions in Malaysia as a whole. I then examine differences in the structural and institutional factors in the state of Penang and see whether these differences lead to the policy environment and economic governance institutions predicted by the theory.

4.1 Malaysia (1957–1969)

4.1.1 Constraints

Systemic Vulnerability: Malaya achieved full independence from the British in 1957. Throughout colonial rule, British administrators had brought in Chinese and Indians to work as laborers and allowed economic function

Table 4.1 Vulnerability and number of veto players in Malaysia and Penang

	1957–1969	*1970–2008*
Malaysia	One Veto PlayerModerate Vulnerability	One Veto PlayerLow Vulnerability
Penang		One Veto PlayerHigh Vulnerability

to become strongly associated with ethnicity. At the time of independence, the country's largest ethnic groups were Malays (49%), Chinese (37%), and Indians (11%) (Hai 2002, 102). Poorer Malays largely worked in agriculture while elites were officials and administrators. Poor Chinese and Indians tended to work as laborers in mines and plantations while elites managed tax farms and opened shops and companies. By the time of independence this economic stratification had become highly entrenched and was resented, particularly by Malay groups.

A Communist insurgency, made up primarily of Chinese laborers, had plagued the Malayan peninsula since World War II. The British mobilized and worked alongside the Malayan Communist Party (MCP) to combat Japanese forces in the war and were unable to prevent them from filling the political vacuum after the Japanese surrender. Well organized and angered by elite Malay complicity with Japanese anti-Chinese activities, Chinese communists targeted Malays for retribution, triggering a spiral of inter-communal violence. In addition to armed hostilities with the largely Chinese communists in the jungle and MCP-sponsored assassinations in the cities, mass inter-communal rioting occurred in this period (Slater 2005, 221–232).

Eventually, under British direction and with the active participation of elites from each of the main ethnic groups, the communists were isolated and marginalized. But resentments over economic stratification had been brought to the surface and the fear of large-scale inter-communal violence made the newly independent government of Malaya extremely wary of any mass unrest. The Alliance coalition that formed the first government, though undoubtedly elite-focused, reached across ethnic and class lines for support.

The British left Malaya on relatively amicable terms and peninsular Malaya only shared a land border with anti-communist Thailand to the North. In 1961, again with British support, Malaya proposed to join with Sabah, Sarawak, Brunei, and Singapore to form Malaysia. Non-aligned Indonesia labeled this plan a form of British sponsored neocolonialism and initiated a period of *Konfrontasi* (confrontation). The confrontation consisted mainly of small-scale raids and the attempted mobilization of communist forces across the potential federation partners (Sutter 1966, 527–531). With British help, the governments prevented serious destruction and unrest. The Malayan government considered the threat sufficiently severe to enact a tin profit tax to help raise money for defense (Thoburn 1978, 33). With the exception of Brunei, the former colonies joined to form the Federation of Malaysia in 1963. Singapore was ejected from the federation 2 years later.

Ethnic considerations were key to the formation of the federation and the ejection of Singapore. The desire to prevent Singapore from falling into the hands of the Communists was key to Malayan Prime Minister Tunku Abdul Rahman's willingness to join with Singapore. But inclusion of the island's predominantly Chinese population would have tilted the scales of power decidedly away from the Malays and UMNO. By welcoming Sabah and Sarwak, the Tunku was able to balance the incoming Chinese with the indigenous peoples of those regions. Once a part of the federation, however, Singapore's People's Action Party (PAP) challenged the Alliance's policy of limited privileges for Malays and UMNO began campaigning in Singapore. Ethnic and political tensions worsened sufficiently to prompt the Tunku to change his mind and expel the island from the federation in 1965.

Natural resources were an important part of the Malaysian economy in this period. Primary commodities made up 80% of total exports in 1960, led by rubber (55.5%), tin (14%), timber (5.4%), petroleum (4%), and palm oil (1.7%) (Andaya and Andaya 2001, 295). Tin exports provided an average of 6% of fiscal revenue between 1955 and 1976 but rubber remained the main revenue earner for the government (Van Lam 1978, 434; Rudner 1994, 134). A sustained reduction in world rubber prices throughout the 1960s hurt government revenues but was partially offset by an upswing in tin prices and an increase in taxes on tin (Van Lam 1978, 443). These resources provided the government with an important, though limited, budgetary cushion as it resolved internal ethnic conflicts and met external threats (Fig. 4.1).

Malaysia experienced severe sensitivity to unrest, limited external threats, and moderate resource levels. Vulnerability was thus moderate prior to 1969.

Veto Players: Malaysia has a bi-cameral legislature, with the upper house invested with the power to delay, not block, legislation. Though it has a parliamentary system with several parties, two successive coalitions led by the UMNO have dominated the Malaysian political scene since 1954: the Alliance between 1954 and 1973, BN after that. In the period between independence and 1969, the Alliance functioned as something between a single political party and a coalition of parties. Though the MCA had some substantial influence within the party, coalition members did not compete directly with each other and UMNO had a dominant

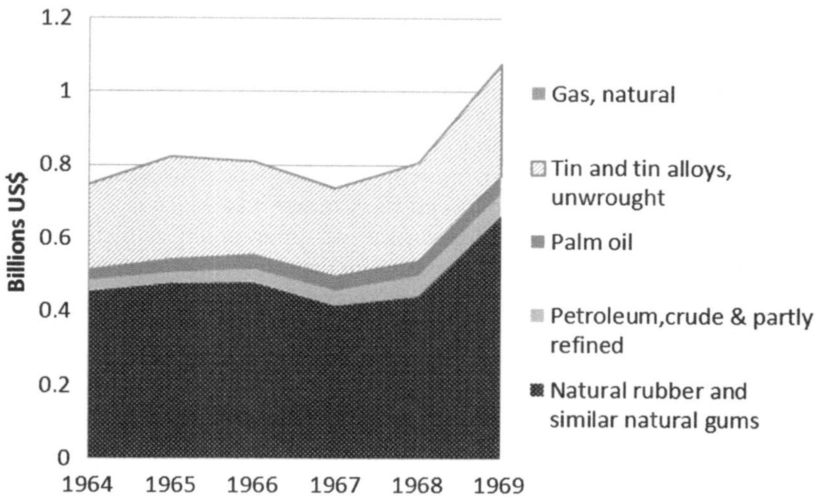

Fig. 4.1 Value of primary commodity exports in Malaysia (1964–1969) Source: (Hai 2002, 129)

position relative to its coalition partners. As such I treat it as a single veto player government.

The MCA clearly played a key role in formulating economic policy in this period.[1] Members of MCA and the larger Chinese community played many critical roles for the coalition. MCA President Tan Siew Sin served as Minister of Commerce and Industry from 1957 to 1961 and Minister of Finance after 1959. The Associated Chinese Chamber of Commerce president H.S. Lee played a significant role in formulating free-market stance espoused in election pledges. The MCA also bankrolled election expenses for the coalition.

Despite the importance of the MCA, the Alliance coalition that ruled Malaysia after independence is better thought of as a single veto player government for two key reasons. First, the constituent parties did not compete with each other for seats in federal elections. Before each election, the UMNO leadership would decide which seats would be contested by each of the member parties.[2] UMNO, the MCA, and the Malaysian Indian Congress (MIC) each competed for seats with opposition parties from within their respective ethnic groups but did not compete with each other. Second, deep concerns about violence toward non-Malays led ethnic Chinese elites to be wary of challenging UMNO's dominance in the coalition. Chinese economic preeminence throughout and after British rule had led to considerable resentment among ethnic Malays which had led to violence both before and after independence. These fissures widened as the anti-communist struggle in pre-independence Malaya led to violent inter-communal riots between the Chinese and Malays.

Malay preeminence in the legislature was guaranteed at first by gerrymandering, strict citizenship requirements, and mal-apportionment in favor of rural, Malay-dominated regions (Hai 2002, 123–124). Over time, a consistently higher Malay population growth rate gave it an ever larger portion of the population, from just over half in 1964 to 65% in 2000 (Brown 2005, 430). This meant that, within the coalition, UMNO had enough electoral muscle to dictate the coalition's policies. Previously moderate levels of gerrymandering and strategic mal-apportionment were expanded by UMNO (Brown 2005, 435). Table 4.2 shows the sizable jump in delineation advantage in the 1974 elections, the first after the 1969 riots.

With moderate levels of vulnerability and one veto player, the typological framework employed here predicts that Malaysia should have a stable policy environment with a mix of broadly and narrowly targeted policies.

Table 4.2 Malay electoral advantage in peninsular Malaysia

Year	*1955*	*1959*	*1964*	*1969*	*1974*	*1986*	*1994*	*1999*
% Malay in population	49.8	50	50	52.9	53.2	55.2	58.1	59.3
% Malay in electorate	84.2	57.1	54.4	55.7	57.9	55.3	56.3	56.7
% Malay-majority constituencies	96.2	57.7	56.7	57.7	69.3	69.7	67.4	68.1
Enfranchisement advantage	34.4	7.1	4.4	2.8	4.7	0.1	−1.8	−2.6
Delineation advantage	12	0.6	2.3	2	11.4	14.4	11.1	11.4
Total Electoral advantage	46.4	7.7	6.7	4.8	16.1	14.5	9.3	8.8

Source (Hai 2002)

4.1.2 Policy Environment

Macroeconomic Policy: Since independence, macroeconomic policy has been set by the central government in Kuala Lumpur. Prior to 1969, the Alliance pursued a relatively non-interventionist industrial policy, aside from import substitution tariffs and some basic infrastructure. This approach placed few demands upon government revenues. Monetary policy was geared toward maintaining price stability, with relatively stable interest rates throughout the 1960s (Young et al. 1980, 37, 159–165). Maintaining the value of the Ringgit was another policy objective that was successfully achieved.[3] Inflation was kept under 1% annually through the 1960s, despite an average 5.2% annual real expansion of GDP (Sheng 1989, 6).

Sectoral Policy: Economic actors in Malaysia faced a stable, broadly targeted sectoral policy environment in the period following independence. Sectoral intervention was not seen as an effective way to meet the government's policy objectives. Though some industries were targeted with promotion, it took the form of tariffs along an import-substitution strategy and there was very little targeting of specific companies in industry (Rasiah and Shari 2001, 59). These policies contributed little to the expansion of the manufacturing sector and the government finally reoriented toward export markets, starting with the Investments Incentive Act in 1968. The policies directed at improving the lot of poor Malays remained "low-key and gradualistic" in this period and were primarily focused on agriculture (Heng 1998, 39).

Overall the policy environment was both broadly targeted and predictable in this period. As such the framework predicts that economic governance institutions will be coordinated.

4.1.3 Economic Governance Institutions

Corporate Governance Institutions: Immediately after independence the Malaysian economy was dominated by foreign capital, particularly in resource extraction. The Malaysian capital market was important to the economy though largely dominated by the British. As seen in Table 4.3, the foreign share of Malaysian companies was 60% overall even as late as the 1970s. In mining, agriculture, and forestry, where British firms were still dominant, the foreign share was nearly 75%.

Table 4.3 Peninsular Malaysia: Ownership of share capital

Sector	*Total*	*Foreign*	*Foreign Share*
	RM mil.	*RM mil.*	*%*
Agriculture, forestry and fisheries	1432.4	1079.7	75.4
Mining and quarrying	543.5	393.9	72.5
Manufacturing	1348.2	804.36	59.7
Construction	58.4	19.9	34.1
Transport and communications	81.9	9.8	12.0
Commerce	605.2	384.5	63.5
Banking and insurance	636.9	332.8	52.3
Others	582.5	182.9	31.4
Total	5289	3207.9	60.7

Source Mid-term Review of the Second Malaysia Plan 1971–1975. Reproduced from Hirschman (n.d.)

Of the firms owned by Malaysians, most were either small Chinese family firms or large family-centered conglomerates. Over the course of the period, Chinese entrepreneurs had moved from retailing to wholesaling, importing, and exporting. Most of the firms in manufacturing were small-scale and family-run (Gomez 2009, 354). Chinese firms also moved into light manufacturing in import-substituting industries such as textiles, shoes, and garments (Giroud 2003, 105). The more successful of these expanded into new sectors including resource extraction, property, and banking (Searle 1998, 37–38). These large conglomerates, largely centered on successful Chinese families established themselves as major players and they diversified across many sectors of the economy (Gomez 2009, 368).

There were few significant Malay entrepreneurs in manufacturing throughout this period. Those Malays that became active in business were mainly in timber, mining, transportation, and contracting. "These were sectors where the federal and state governments had a strong say over entry…and could thus favour Malay applicants, especially their friends and kin. Many of the Malays who entered these sectors were encouraged by their good access to government officials and enticed by the quick money to be made" (Jesudason 1989, 66).

The Malaysian government, seeking to promote ownership among ethnic Malays established the National Investment Company in 1961. Malays were allowed to buy into the company, which would in turn buy shares of firms that received Pioneer status. That only $3.8 million out of $15.1 million worth of allocated shares were purchased demonstrates the limited savings capacity among Malays at the time (Jesudason 1989, 64–65).

Banks and other institutional investors representing patient capital were not important sources of funding for firms in this period. As seen in Table 4.4, shares of banks made up less than one-tenth of one percent of the total value of all financial companies in Malaysia in 1972.

Firms built around Chinese individual and family owners dominated the period, the most powerful of which were "Kuala Lumpur-Kepong (Lee Loy Seng), Federal Flour (Robert Kuok), Asia Motor Co. (Phang family), Cycle and Carriage (Chua family), Lee Rubber Selangor (Lee family), Tan Chong Motors (Tan family), EmpatNomborEkor (Lim family) and Hock Heng Co. (Ng family)" (Gomez 2009, 352). A survey of ownership in the early 1970s found a very high degree of ownership concentration: "The top 1% of these 797 shareholders owned 29% of this equity, while the top 50% owned 97% and the bottom 20% only 0.4%" (Gomez 2009).

Overall, the period featured a mix of hierarchical and liberal corporate governance institutions. The capital market was robust but dominated by large foreign firms and small family firms. There was no evidence of the strong coordinative governance institutions suggested by the stable, broadly targeted policy environment.

Table 4.4 Ordinary shareholdings by types of Malaysian financial companies

Type of Financial Company	*Number*	*Shareholdings* %	*Value in thousands of USD*	*Shareholdings Percentage* %
Investment Companies	529	52.7	106,721.9	90.2
Insurance Companies	96	9.6	7308.7	6.2
Trust Bodies	366	36.5	4065.2	3.5
Banks	12	1.2	167.0	0.1
Total	1003	100	118,262.8	100

Source 1972 Financial Survey of Limited Companies, Department of Statistics, Malaysia. Reproduced from Ling (2005)

Inter-firm Relations: The main form of inter-firm linkages existed among ethnic Chinese entrepreneurs. Coordination was limited to areas of common interest. "Compared to the Malays, Chinese had superior access to capital and credit through their associations, and Chambers of Commerce which were established in Malaya after 1906. These organizations served as networks for members to gather and exchange information on market conditions, and as sources of credit and capital for starting or expanding one's business" (Hicken 2007).

4.1.4 Electrical/Electronics Industries

Corporate Governance Institutions: Electronics was one of the sectors designated as 'pioneering' for the purposes of promotion. The blanket nature of protection however meant that promotion policies were relatively broadly targeted. These broadly targeted policies were also stable over the period and not subject to radical shifts.

As in Thailand, local Chinese firms acted as distributors for Japanese electrical appliance multinationals through the 50s and 60s. Japanese manufacturers Sanyo and Matsushita took on Malaysian investors in establishing manufacturing operations. In 1966 Matsushita listed Matsushita Electric Company (later Panasonic Manufacturing Malaysia Berhad) on the Kuala Lumpur Stock Exchange and offered 50% of the equity to Malaysian investors. The company produced a variety of electrical appliances. Other EEI producers were established in other states, including Sanyo (50% held by Malaysians) in Taiping.

Inter-firm Linkage Institutions: As most firms were run by ethnic Chinese families in this period, inter-firm linkages were primarily limited to small networks based on the regions of China from which the families originated. There is little information on the makeup and activities of peak business associations and other forms of inter-firm linkage institutions in this period.

4.2 Malaysia (1969–2008)

The 1969 elections were a tremendous setback for the ruling Alliance party. Though they retained control of the legislature due to gerrymandering and malapportionment, they garnered only 48.4% of the vote. Additionally, they lost control of the state leadership in Penang and tied with the opposition in Selangor. Chinese opposition celebrations and parades triggered counter-demonstrations by Alliance supporters and eventually riots spread throughout Kuala Lumpur and other cities with large numbers of Chinese. The resulting rioting and arson, according to official figures, left nearly two-hundred dead and thousands homeless. In the aftermath of the riots the government declared a state of emergency and suspended parliament.

4.2.1 Constraints

Systemic Vulnerability: Systemic vulnerability remained moderately low at the federal level during this period. Cold-war tensions were sufficiently distant from Malaysia's borders to limit the budgetary demands of its defense needs. Though concern over the domestic communist threat had diminished significantly by 1969, the ethnic riots made it clear to UMNO leaders that they would need to reach out more to the rural Malay majority. Indeed, ensuring that ethnic hostilities were contained became the overriding goal of the Alliance/BN coalition.

Malaysia became a net oil exporter in the mid-1970s, with the federal government controlling revenues thanks to the 1974 Petroleum Development Act. The government also controlled Petronas, the state-owned oil company (Jomo and Gomez 2000, 280). These, together with tin, rubber, natural gas, and palm oil exports (see Figs. 4.2 and4.3) gave the government considerable revenue with which to keep its broad coalition together. Particularly from the mid-1970s on, the government was freed from budgetary constraints and could provide narrowly targeted side payments.

Global commodity prices dropped substantially in the mid-1980s, especially in crude oil and palm oil (Sheng 1989, 7). Crude oil prices fell 62% from its peak. Total export income was reduced by 2.6% in 1985 and 5.9% in 1986 (Sheng 1989, 9). The price of crude oil has tripled since 2003 and the value of Malaysian petroleum-related exports have increased by a factor of five ("UN Comtrade" 2012) (Figs. 4.2 and 4.3).

Thus, after 1969 Malaysia faced low systemic vulnerability. The increase in inter-ethnic tensions was more than offset by the dramatic growth of the revenue base from natural resources, and the decline of the regional and internal communist threat.

Veto Players: Once the violence of the 1969 riots subsided and elections were restored, the MCA was even more acquiescent to UMNO domination of the coalition. The specter of future mass anti-Chinese

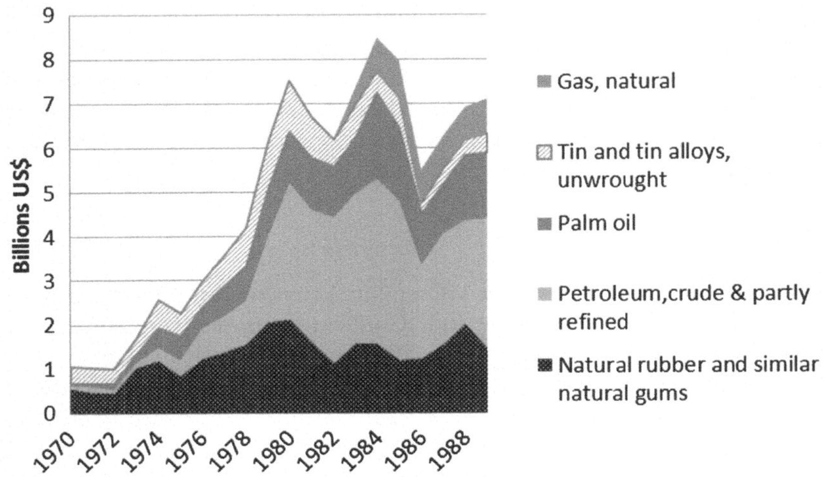

Fig. 4.2 Value of primary commodity exports in Malaysia (1970–1989) *Source* UN Comtrade Database

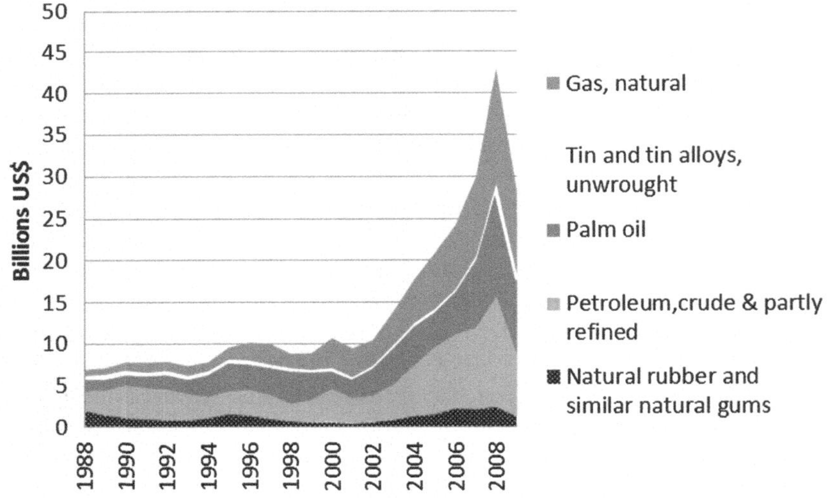

Fig. 4.3 Value of resource exports in Malaysia (1989–2014) *Source* UN Comtrade Database

violence, potentially backed by the Malaysian state, was enough to largely silence MCA opposition to UMNO's policy agenda. The new BN coalition represented a collective actor that was much more hierarchically organized, with the UMNO leadership at the top.[4]

With the MCA unwilling to provoke UMNO and Malay violence, it could not threaten to withdraw from the coalition and therefore lacked effective veto power. As such, I treat the federal government as a single veto player for both macroeconomic and sectoral policy areas. It is worth noting here that I am saying that the MCA political party after 1969 is not a veto player while the factions within Thai political parties are. Though this seems counterintuitive, I feel that the following facts support that assessment. First, the MCA did not directly oppose UMNO in elections while various factions within Thai political parties did compete; second, particularly after the 1969 riots, the MCA could not credibly threaten to leave the coalition while Thai factions did; third, there was a relatively clear organizational structure in which MCA was fundamentally beneath UMNO while the relationship among factions in Thai political parties were much more fluid (MacIntyre 2003b, 43, 44).

Major rifts emerged in UMNO itself on two occasions. In the early-mid 1980s the rise of new Malay capitalists (described below) associated with PM Mahathir and Daim Zainuddin led former Finance Minister Razaleigh Hamzah to challenge Mahathir for control of UMNO. Mahathir maintained control and Hamzah's faction joined the oppositon in a nearly successful effort to unseat BN in the next election (Gomez 2002, 97). In the mid 1990s, UMNO again felt threatened by division within the Malay community and sought greater non-Bumiputera support. But rather than restoring the MCA's institutionalized power within BN, PM Mahathir expanded the distribution of narrowly targeted policy benefits to Chinese and Indian businessmen such as Vincent Tan, Ting PekKhiing, and T. Ananda Krishnan (Gomez 2002, 91).

With low vulnerability and one, non-alternating veto player, the typological framework predicts that Selangor should be highly particularistic in the post-1969 period.

4.2.2 Policy Environment

Macroeconomic Policy: The macroeconomic policy environment faced by economic actors after the 1969 crisis was less stable and more narrowly targeted. Because UMNO sought to meet its redistribution and growth goals by intervening much more directly in the market, other goals such as price and exchange rate stability and fiscal prudence were somewhat compromised.

Annual inflation rose from under 1% in the 1960s to an average of 6% in the 1970s (Sheng 1989, 6). In the mid-1970s, the government sought to counteract the drop in demand for Malaysian products brought about by a global downturn by increasing its capital expenditures even though revenues were stagnating (Narayanan 1996, 871). The dramatic increase in the value of exported natural resources in the late 1970s allowed the government to drastically expand its role in the economy.[5] Expenditures underwent a substantial expansion as PM Mahathir Mohamad attempted to create a Malaysian heavy industry program and create a new class of Malay businessmen (more below).

In 1981, shortly before elections, the government announced that its commitment to the fiscal requirements of the NEP was of paramount importance and it would continue with planned spending increases, despite the global downturn that occurred in the early 1980s. The following year it reversed itself and announced that it would trim spending by 30% on account of the recession. In the end, it was reduced by only 10%. Budget deficits rose from 8.3% in 1980 to 18.7% of GNP by 1982. Figure 4.4 shows the growing deficits in this period. Likewise, the current account deficit rose from 1.1% to 14% (Narayanan 1996, 873). The off-budget agencies tasked with implementing NEP objectives continued to have their budgets increased even as other forms of development spending was slashed.

After 1984, the federal government switched policy tracks altogether and began reducing the direct role of the government in the economy. This led to a gradual decline in the budget allocations for the NEP's off-budget agencies. Substantial tax reforms were also enacted in the mid-80s including large tax cuts along a supply-side framework (Fig. 4.5).

The onset of the 1997 economic crisis simulated several shifts in policy. The ringgit (RM) dropped from 2.52 to the dollar in June 1997 to 3.2 to the dollar in September, and 4.5 the following January. The value of the stock market also dropped rapidly as investors sought firm ground. Especially in trouble were those firms that had substantial foreign debt valued in other currencies. The government response included substantial policy changes and reversals (MacIntyre 2003b, 82–90). There was a power struggle over economic policy between PM Mahathir who championed an expansionary policy with restrictions on capital movements

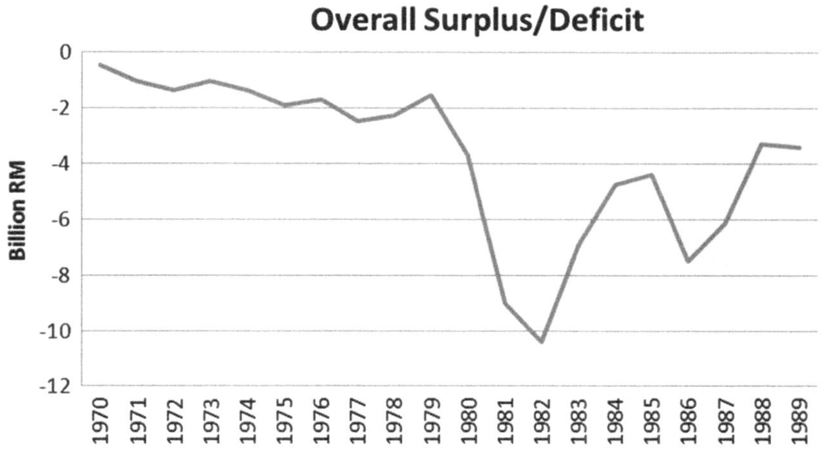

Fig. 4.4 Malaysian government deficit (1970–1989) *Source* Malaysiam Ministry of Finance

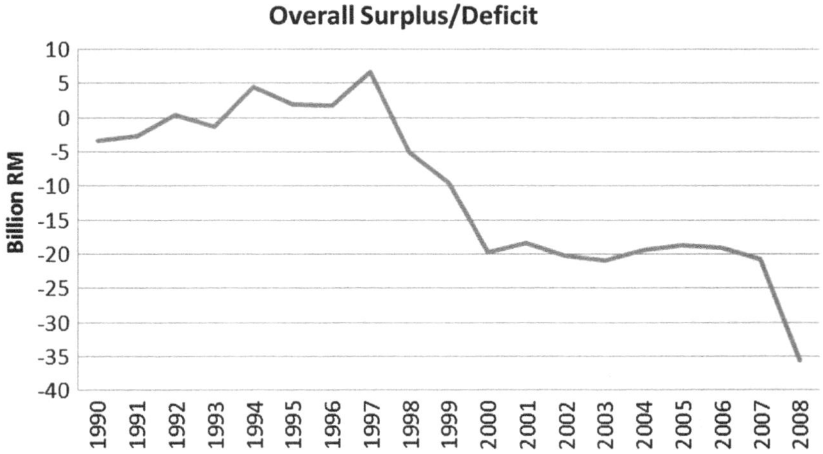

Fig. 4.5 Malaysian government deficit (1990–2008) *Source* Malaysian Ministry of Finance

and Deputy PM Anwar Ibrahim who favored a more orthodox approach. The government went back and forth between the two approaches until Anwar was sacked and arrested. In the end, the government imposed selective capital controls and pegged the ringgit to the dollar. Additionally, the group, led by the PM, created several bodies to take on non-performing loans and assets and to help banks recapitalize (Ping and Yean 2007, 917). This allowed the government to both pursue an expansionary macroeconomic policy by lowering interest rates and shelter Mahathir's supporters in the corporate sector (Ping and Yean 2007; Johnson and Mitton 2003; Johnson 2006). In the following decade the government made adjustments to these policies, loosening restrictions on portfolio investment in 2001 and dismantling the peg in 2005 (Ping and Yean 2007, 921).

Sectoral Policy: The sectoral policy environment faced by economic actors after the tumult of the 1969 riots was narrowly targeted. The Malaysian government introduced the New Economic Policy (NEP) to reduce inter-ethnic tensions by improving the lot of Malays. This new policy vastly expanded the scope of government intervention in the economy, with the stated goal of increasing the Bumiputras' stake in the economy to 30% by 1991. Public sector and education quotas for Malays were expanded and new affirmative requirements were instituted for all new IPOs. In addition, the Malaysian government, on behalf of the Malay people, sponsored and subsidized sectors and businesses directly through a wide array of government institutions including MARA (Council of Trust For The Indigenous People), the Urban Development Authority (UDA), and PERNAS (National Trading Corporation), each of which formed many subsidiary organizations and joint ventures. While the thrust of these initiatives was reducing the association between ethnicity and economic function and not industrial policy as such, the practical result was a sharp increase in the availability of narrowly targeted policies.

These policies gave preferential treatment to those with access, particularly UMNO loyalists, including: subsidized financing, government contracts, state-owned enterprises (SOE) and SOE subsidiary procurements, and regulatory assistance (Syn 2002, 15). The government was the largest buyer of goods and service, with public consumption and investment totaling around 30% of GDP (Jesudason 1989, 92). It used this buying power to favor Malay businesses, particularly those with access. Finance was a key mechanism designed to increase the share of Malay capitalists. The government sought to achieve this by both directly holding companies and shares of companies in trust for the Malay people and by helping specific Malays acquire or establish companies of their own.

A number of government bodies were created to these ends. The funds that were made available to (largely) Malay companies came with little oversight and were distributed first and foremost to those with political access.

> Two mechanisms critical for the rapid ascent of the Malay bourgeoisie were access "from strong connections and political links" to enormous funds from the banking system (especially state-controlled and state-owned banks), and state regulatory power, which enabled Malays to buy cheap shares using borrowed money as a key to capital accumulation. (Jesudason 1989, 105)

Licensing was also used to favor Malay businesses. In 1975, the government sought to tighten up licensing requirements that were being bypassed by Chinese firms by passing the Industrial Coordination Act. The act substantially expanded the scope of federal oversight of individual firm decisions. Enforcement of the licensing requirements was erratic (as the economy worsened immediately following the passage of the act the government backed off on some provisions) and at times used to assist *bumiputra* firms with access.

In the early 1970s, the federal government funneled money into State Economic Development Corporations (SEDC). Tasked with promoting NEP goals and economic development at the local level, the institutions were largely another means of distributing narrow policy benefits. "The chief ministers and local politicians who sat on the SEDC boards pushed for projects that would extend their patronage and enhance their political fortunes, paying little attention to economic rationality...This form of parasitism on state resources led to a situation in which SEDC officers were highly reluctant to close down companies which were making large losses until central authorities forced them to do so" (Jesudason 1989, 99).

Prime Minister Dr. Mahathir Mohamad pursued a heavy industry policy upon coming to power in 1981. His government promoted Malaysian steel, petrochemical, and automobile industries by creating the Heavy Industries Corporation of Malaysia (HICOM).

UMNO's goal of eliminating the association of ethnicity and class had, by the mid-1980s been achieved insomuch as a new group of Malay capitalists had been created. This group, which had risen thanks to their ability to access policy-makers, sought to expand the semi-private portion of the market that was out of direct control of the bureaucracy but was still eligible for UMNO's support (Syn 2002, 27). With the poor performance of the public enterprises clearly evident by this time, the government indulged this new Malay bourgeoisie and began to privatize some of the SOEs.[6] Though the privatization that occurred under Dr. Mahathir changed the form that narrowly targeted policies took, it did not diminish the overall amount of these policies. Indeed, the manner in which SOEs and SOE subsidiaries were sold off and the manner in which state-controlled investment funds, held in trust for the Malay people, were redistributed to private hands were especially collusive.

In addition to privatization, Dr. Mahathir's government sought to foster greater technology development under the 'Vision 2020' program. Starting in the mid-1980s, the government effectively streamlined and coordinated the activities of the various bureaucratic agencies responsible for sectoral policy formation and implementation (Felker 1998a). Another part of the program involved the improvement of public–private consultative mechanisms. Although several such bodies were created and served as focal points for the implementation of government programs, communication was largely one-way. Rather than engaging peak business organizations, the government selected specific business leaders to participate in bodies like the Malaysian Business Council and MIGHT that were chaired by the PM or cabinet members directly. The government's various policy goals and programs were then communicated to the participants. One executive participating in MIGHT noted, "It's just like a talk-shop so far, but we have no choice but to show up and listen" (Felker 1998a, 163).

As mentioned above, the 1997 crisis threatened many in the corporate sector. The government's policy responses served to shelter UMNO supporters. Government funds flowed through new institutions to bolster the banking sector and free up credit, but favored connected firms. Distressed firms with connections were also bailed out by the state-owned oil company and were assisted by new contracts with the government (Ping and Yean 2007; Johnson and Mitton 2003; Johnson 2006).

The two administrations that have led Malaysia since the departure of Dr. Mahathir have largely followed the same trajectory at the national level. Ambitious, well-constructed economic plans have identified a pathway to continued development through industrial upgrading but the lack of autonomy and embeddedness has systematically undermined these efforts at the federal level.

Between Abdullah Badawi's 2003 rise to the premiership and the 2004 national elections, the government pursued an aggressive campaign to combat corruption. Spending on major infrastructure projects was cut and a few high-profile politicians associated with former PM Mahathir were prosecuted for corruption (Burton 2004). After the election, however, there was significant resistance from Dr. Mahathir and powerful factions within UMNO, undermining Badawi's position and the anti-corruption campaign (Case 2008; Lopez 2004). The remainder of Badawi's administration was troubled by abuse of power allegations: one of the largest anti-corruption cases of the pre-election drive was dismissed, a scandal emerged involving then deputy PM Najib Razak's security team and the murder of a Mongolian model, a video was released showing the fixing of judicial appointments, and allegations of corruption were targeted at Badawi's Anti-Corruption Agency (Singh 2009). Additionally, Badawi's early promise to steer policy away from pork-laden, large infrastructure projects was abandoned.

The Najib administration has also suffered from several high-profile corruption cases and perception of corruption levels has worsened. Public trust in the government's anti-corruption efforts was further undermined when an opposition political aid from Selangor was found dead outside of the Malaysian Anti-Corruption Commission. A subsequent inquest organized by the Selangor state government suggested that the aid was murdered. Many speculated that he died while the federal government was pressing him aggressively for information that might discredit the opposition government in Selangor (Chin 2010). Allegations have linked the death of the Mongolian model to government kickbacks received during substantial defense purchases (Martin 2012). Thus, in the 10 years since Dr. Mahathir's departure the politicians have demonstrated little willingness to reign in corruption.

Various comparative surveys of corruption perception reflect these broad trends. The World Bank's World Governance Indicators, a set of composite indicators based on a wide variety of data sources, includes an assessment of 'control of corruption' for countries over time. This indicator ranges from -2.5 (corruption is not controlled) to 2.5 (corruption is well controlled). Control of corruption "captures perceptions of the extent to which public power is exercised for private gain, including both petty and grand forms of corruption, as well as "capture" of the state by elites and private interest" (Kaufmann et al. 2012). As can be seen in Fig. 4.6, there is an uptick in the perception that the government is working to control corruption in 2003 and 2004 but then a downward trend.

Transparency International's Global Corruption Barometer shows a similar pattern in perception of the level of corruption in specific government institutions; since 2008 there has been an increase in the perception that Parliament and the Judiciary are corrupt (World Corruption Barometer 2012). Critically, Transparency International's *Putting Corruption out of Business* survey found that 50% of those firms surveyed thought that they had failed to win a government contract because a competitor paid a bribe—the highest percentage in the countries surveyed (World Corruption Barometer 2012).

Overall, the economic policy environment in the 1969–2013 period was narrowly targeted and featured moderate volatility. Three major policy shifts occurred: the shift to exports that had begun in 1968 coupled with execution of the NEP, the shift to heavy industrialization and privatization. Thus, without strong systemic pressures, the Malaysian

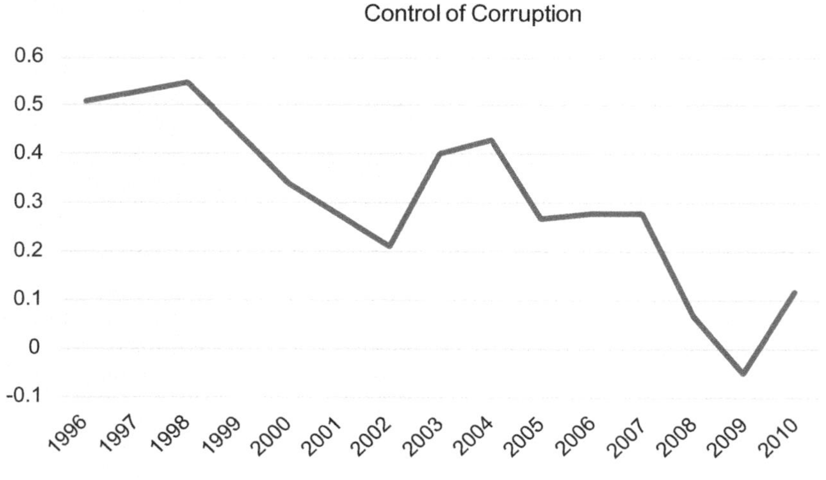

Fig. 4.6 Control of corruption in Malaysia *Source* World Bank's World Governance Indicators

government has not been compelled to insulate economic policy implementation from political and patronage concerns.

4.2.3 Economic Governance Institutions

Corporate Governance Institutions: Corporate governance institutions were predominantly hierarchical in Malaysia during this period. The dominant forms of corporate governance were Chinese-owned diversified family conglomerates and government owned, sponsored, or funded Malay corporations.

The post-1969 period featured a significant expansion of the formal liberal corporate governance institutions. Malaysia had one of the most sophisticated financial systems in the developing world (Sheng 1989, 7). These formal institutions were, however, largely altered to meet the needs of private actors whose incentives were primarily driven by the hierarchical policy environment. The size of the national exchange increased dramatically over this period but much of this expansion was due to government and quasi-government bodies using the capital markets to intervene in markets, boost Malay ownership, and expand UMNO's influence. Foreign investors, though numerous, did not engage local JV partners to the same degree that they did in Thailand (Felker 1998a). Family-owned Chinese diversified conglomerates (more below) also made use of the national stock market but retained ownership and control.

There were no substantial coordinative corporate governance institutions operating in Malaysia outside of Penang at this time. Several large government-sponsored funds and one private Chinese fund had the potential to act as patient capital but tended to allocate capital based on access rather than long-term market share.

The Chinese MCA attempted to form a holding company in 1975 in order to facilitate the transformation of small, family firms into modern corporations. The Multi-Purpose Holdings Berhad (MPHB) was to allow Chinese members to pool their resources and benefit from stronger coordination among their firms. In 1977 it had raised $30 million in the stock market, with 40% of its equity held by middle class Chinese through the MCA Youth Cooperative Society. The company quickly grew to be one of the largest on the KLSE, despite the fact that the most powerful Chinese families, with their own ties to policy-makers in UMNO, did not participate. Coordination was weak, however, and corruption was rampant in the management of the fund (Searle 1998, 177–188). The recession of the mid-1980s hit MPHB hard and the MCA sold its shares to the Lim family's Kamunting Group 1989. After its demise, large Chinese conglomerates expanded their efforts to gain access to UMNO officials. "In reality the most common feature among Chinese enterprises during the NEP period was that of extensive and intensive competition for limited resources between them rather than intra-ethnic cooperatio" (Gomez 2008, 97). This pattern of low coordination among Chinese family conglomerates and competition for political access continued into the 2000s (Gomez 2008).

In the 1970s, UMNO created holding companies and business groups, including Fllet Holdings, Hatibudi, Halimtan, and Koperasi. In the early 1980s, after resource revenues stimulated the scope and scale of government intervention in the economy, these companies, with the exception of Halimtan, used easy access to government credit and preferential access to special Bumiputera shares to expand their activities and grow. They developed cross-shareholding structures in the mid-1980s but largely to hide UMNO's role (Searle 1998, 104–118). In the early 1990s, the party moved away from direct ownership but high ranking UMNO politicians retained significant holdings and management positions in important firms throughout the economy (Gomez 2002, 99).

Several venture capital funds were established in this period, though they differed considerably from the operations of either Western venture funds or funds operating in Singapore.[7] By 1999, there was $667 million available. The largest portion of these funds, 45% came from government agencies. Thirty percent came from corporations and 17% came from banks (Kenney et al. 2002, 122). In addition to the "crowding out" of private investment, the government funds often sent distorting signals to the market, with ethnic and political objectives quite independent of growth or profitability. In this context, firm governance and finance tended to be based on loyalty ties rather than on either publicly available information on short-term profits or long-term market share prospects. As such, family firms and firms built around political patronage channels were dominant.

The unsatisfactory performance of government-supported firms together with the loss of Malay support for UMNO in the early 1990s motivated PM Mahathir to reorient government policy towards finding and supporting local firms that would be more successful in the export market. Initiatives were undertaken to provide capital to Malaysian entrepreneurs for that purpose. The Malaysia Technology Development

Corporation (MTDC), with paid-up capital of US$20 million, was created in 1991 to fund the development and commercialization of government research (Felker 1998b, 169). When the private sector did not engage the project, the MTDC provided seed money more generally, controlling six funds worth US$200 million by 1996. The organization developed a reputation of being relatively "non-political." The fund did not, however, operate like patient capital common to CMEs, directly guiding business activities. One of the MTDC portfolio company's owner/managers noted that they normally "seek a minority shareholding of not more than 30% and would not interfere with the day-to-day operation of the company. We do not have the slightest intention to run the entrepreneur's business" (Felker 1998b, 208). For the most part it provided Chinese firms a source of neutral Malay-originating investment funds that met the NEP's 30% requirements but would not interfere in their operations.

Family owned and managed diversified conglomerates were the dominant form of corporate governance in Malaysia at this time. As noted above, both the stock market and large party-based funds were used heavily for firms with hierarchical structures. The larger Chinese entrepreneurs maintained and expanded their businesses by gaining access to influential Malays in UMNO, the bureaucracy and the Malay royalty. "During the NEP, Chinese entrepreneurs relied even more on their Malay business partners to gain access to business opportunities which came under the purview of state institutions. The most successful Chinese entrepreneurs were those with powerful Malay patrons" (Heng 1998, 50).

Old Groups

Searle characterizes the changes that occurred in the structure of Chinese business groups before and after the NEP, indicating the move toward greater diversification as a more particularistic policy environment emerges (Searle 1998). Table 4.5 reports Searle's findings. Overall, this reflects a shift toward more ideal-typical hierarchical corporate governance institutions in this period.

Inter-firm Relations: The horizontal and vertical relationships among firms in Malaysia were limited and hierarchical. The government preferred to interact with businesses by creating informal bodies with key business leaders, such as the Malaysian Business Council, rather than interacting with peak business associations in any institutionalized setting. This both reflected and exacerbated the organizational weakness of private business associations.

Table 4.5 Old vs. New Chinese firms

Old groups	*New groups*
• The growth of the old groups was a 'step-by-step' process, constrained as it was by internally generated sources of finance.	• Rapid growth occurred through dependence on external rather than private or internally generated sources of finance. Principal sources of finance were banks, state funds and the mechanisms of the stock market.
• Old groups were identified with a particular industry (often commodities or construction) as a principal or core activity.	• Investment was in divergent fields rather than concentrated in or identified with one sector or core activity.
• Major Chinese business leaders relied... on a web of personal connections with prominent members of the Malay political elites...political connections and 'clout' for Chinese business came after the accumulation of wealth and was not...a corollary to the process itself.	• Most of the new tycoons are closely associated with a prominent member of the Malay political business elite.

Source Taken from Searle (1998) p. 190 and 222

The largest peak organization, The Federation of Malaysian Manufacturers (FMM) represented the business community but has had a "limited ability to mobilize collective action on a sectoral basis" (Felker 1998b, 107). Some sector-specific ethnic Chinese associations achieved coordination in lobbying the government on trade and tax issues but this led to greater confrontation with the Malay bureaucracy. In general coordination was weak and hierarchical; limited to gaining and retaining patron–client links with UMNO officials.

The government did create programs to directly encourage greater private coordination in the 1980s and 1990s. The effectiveness of these programs was, however, limited by the government's consistently top-down approach and the strong desire of officials to retain discretionary powers over funds. Felker notes that:

> The majority of local private manufacturers, poorly organized to articulate and impress their needs on policy makers, has little access or benefit from government technology incentives. Moreover, many private firms were suspicious of the government's insistence on screening and allocating promotional incentives on a discretionary basis. Quite apart from ethnic political

> issues was a general perception that government discretionary incentives were often used as a tool of patronage. When asked why he had not applied for government incentives, the owner of a successful medium-sized producer of plastic-injection parts replied that '...the government wants to use these programs to play favorites, so we don't bother to apply.' (Felker 1998b, 210)

In 1992, Malaysia's Ministry of International Trade and Industry started a vendor development program that sought to develop local suppliers by strengthening inter-firm linkages. The program provided subsidized credit and other limited benefits to those that took part. MITI would act as a broker, linking local firms with multinationals so as to facilitate the development of local capacities. But, as with other government efforts to facilitate greater private coordination, participation was sparse. One executive from a Chinese business association noted that 'most SMIs do not bother applying because the selection criteria are not transparent, and they assume the participants will be unfairly chosen' (Felker 1998b, 289).

The Malaysian Industry-Government Group for High Technology (MIGHT) was another public–private endeavor created in 1993 to facilitate greater coordination in technological development. As with several other programs in this period, however, private coordination was weak and ineffective, with the body serving more to communicate government objectives than articulating private sector needs (Felker 1998b, 163).

Ethnic Malay associations were used by the government to distribute patronage to medium-sized companies. "In the late 1980s, control of the Malay Chambers and National Chambers of Commerce and Industry was passed to prominent corporate figures selected by Mahathir. Charged with modernizing the associations, the new leadership essentially converted them from moribund vehicles for rent seeking into extensions of the new, high-level clientelist networks which now figured prominently in policy making" (Felker 1998b, 111).

Inter-firm linkage institutions were weak and hierarchically structured in this period. Firms were unwilling to engage with one another and share privately held information, unless through patron–client or familial channels.

4.2.4 Electrical/Electronics Industries

Corporate Governance Institutions: As with the economy more generally, hierarchical corporate governance structures were dominant in the electrical and electronics sectors in Malaysia during this period. Most EEI firms were small Chinese-run firms owned and managed by families or firms with a significant reliance on government programs for financing. The most successful locally owned EEI companies were OYL, MEC, and Sapura.

OYL was established in 1974 by Tun Omar Ong Yoke Lin, a former MCA MP that had served in the cabinet and had been one of the signatories of the agreement establishing Malaysia in London (New Straits Times 2007). Initially producing gas cookers and ovens, OYL expanded in the electrical appliance sector and especially air conditioners. In the following few years OYL formed JVs with Guthrie Malaysia Holdings, Acma, and Borg Warner Corp. TunOng remained the major shareholder until 1990 when the Quek family's powerful Hong Leong group purchased the operation. Infused with new capital, the group ramped up export production, began establishing factories abroad, and acquiring new technologies by purchasing foreign producers such as air-conditioning manufacturers Snyder and AAF-McQuay (Hightower 1994; Select Federal Filings Newswires 1995). In 2006 Japanese air conditioner Daikin purchased the Malaysian multinational (Bisnis Indonesia 2006). The Hong Leong group's other entry into the electronics manufacturing sector, Malaysian Pacific Industries, was created in partnership with the government's Permodalan Nasional Bhd fund in 1985.

MCA Division Chairman Teong TeckLeng's Superior Products Incorporated was established in 1975, producing, among other things, cookware and electrical products. The four Teong brothers expanded operations after acquiring Kuala Lumpur Industries Holdings in 1991 (Pak 1991). The diversified business group was involved in property development and many other activities. They changed the name of Superior Products to Malaysia Electric Corporation (MEC) and expanded operations in 1996, acquiring Australian electrical goods manufacturer Kambrook Distributing (The New Straits Times 1996). MEC worked closely with the Mahathir government to develop the MEC brand and establish the 'MEC City' in Pahang province, with the goal of an electrical appliance cluster (Bernama Infolink Services 1999). It was also enlisted as a major anchor for the government's vendor development program (more below) (New Straits Times 1997). Khazanah, one of the government's investment arms and the state of Pahang were major stakeholders in the MEC City project. The company was badly hurt by Teong's legal troubles starting in 1997 and matters were made worse by the unfolding economic crisis.

Sapura was established by Shamsuddin Abdul Kadir in 1974 as a supplier of telephone equipment to the Malaysian government's telecommunications monopoly. Initially, the firm fed and grew by means of access to powerful government officials, becoming one of the few Bumiputera conglomerates engaged in manufacturing. After resource constraints and privatization led to greater competition for government contracts in the mid-1980s, the company developed its capacities in the industry and expanded its operations without diversifying into several sectors. Searle notes that Sapura was "an outstanding example of a Bumiputra entrepreneur who was not content to rely on good government contracts and contacts but used the initial advantages bestowed by state support to build a strong, dynamic and profitable company…[Shamsuddin] also eschewed profit and growth by expanding into several unrelated sectors of activity, preferring instead to consolidate the group's operations in manufacturing, where he focused in particular on products associated with telecommunications and computer technologies and component parts for vehicle manufacture" (Searle 1998). In addition to utilizing various government pro-Bumiputera financing programs, the Sapura group made heavy use of the stock exchange. It retained control over their core companies but bringing on foreign MNCs for several joint ventures. Though direction of the group was eventually passed to Shamsuddin's son, the firm began bringing professional management in from outside the family in the 1980s (Norsiah Nurani 2001). Sapura thus relied heavily on its access to UMNO officials to acquire finance but did not diversify in ways that sacrificed economies of scale and scope.

Inter-firm Linkage Institutions: As with the rest of the economy, the EEI sector did not engage with the federal government's attempts to promote greater coordination among private companies. The Malaysian Electrical and Electronics Industry Group (MEEIG), the peak electronics association under the FMM was involved primarily in limited lobbying efforts and systematically undermined by the government's informal bodies (K'Zaman 1994). The group is made up of both local and MNC producers such as Asea Brown Boveri, Carrier International, Hitachi, Matsushita, Sanyo, Setron, Sharp-Roxy and OYL Industries.

The electronics sector was made a major part of the government's Vendor Development Program in the early 1990s. Sapura was made an anchor firm in 1992 and given grants to foster the development of local suppliers. Despite these inducements, the linkages were shallow and largely unfruitful. Vendors were unwilling to engage with Sapura and alter their production processes. Sapura vice chairman Rameli Musa said, "We had to practically station our engineers in these factories to teach them everything, from stock control, quality control and production control to sourcing of equipment" (Jacobs 1993). These sorts of problems were widespread in the effort. Ministry of International Trade and Industry's Small and Medium Industries Division director Kassim Sarbani noted, "The main problems faced by vendor companies are operating below capacity, unreasonable price and insufficient guidance from anchor companies. Meanwhile, the problems faced by anchor companies are the supply of inferior quality products, vendors not meeting delivery deadlines and inferior technology of these vendors" (Hamid 1995). But the government was unwilling or unable to help overcome these and other systematic coordinative problems between vendors and anchor firms. In 1996 Entrepreneur Development Minister Datuk Mustapa Mohamed, voiced the government's unhappiness with the development of the problem and told businesses not to make excuses. "There are ways to overcome problems if one exercises positive thinking and is creative enough to seek the best solutions" (Tahir 1996).

Similar conflicts between the government's official goal of strengthening private coordination and its tendency to focus on select businesses while neglecting peak associations were evident in the MEC City project. In 1996 PM Mahathir announced a major push to develop a national producer in the electrical appliance industry. A relatively small electrical appliance firm owned by Kuala Lumpur Industries Holdings (HLIH) was selected as the private partner in the scheme. MEC was to be an anchor firm under the vendor development program and establish strong, information-sharing linkages with local vendors. Without consulting MEEIG, PM Mahathir promised KLIH substantial assistance in addition to subsidized financing and free land. The MEEIG fought the program as it gave MEC substantially greater incentives than were available to existing EEI producers (K'Zaman 1994).

Inter-firm linkage institutions in the electrical and electronics sectors were hierarchical after 1969. Particularistic benefits offered by the federal government through schemes like the vendor development program undermined the possibility of deep coordination in peak institutions. Thus MEEIG was limited to lobbying efforts and had little capacity to resolve collective dilemmas.

4.3 Penang: 1969–2008

4.3.1 Constraints

Systemic Vulnerabilities: Systemic vulnerability is largely analyzed at the national level. Certainly the threat of removal by a foreign power is something that typically occurs at the national level. But the degree to which policy-makers are constrained by the need to appeal to a broad coalition and the degree to which they have easy access to revenue-generating resources can vary from state to state. Likewise, the number of actors empowered to block a change in the policy status quo can vary within a country, particularly within a federal government. State executives and legislatures may have the power to veto policies or policy implementation within their states.

A year before the eruption of ethnic tensions transformed coalitional politics at the federal level, Penang had experienced severe inter-communal violence. Penang's role as an entrepot under the British had diminished significantly during *Konfrontasi*. This was due both to the conflict itself and to the federal government's 2% surtax on Indonesian goods re-exported from Penang (Snider 1968). This led to an estimated 20% unemployment in the state and widespread dissatisfaction. A strike initiated by the opposition Labour Party following a government decision to devalue old currency in circulation led to two months of inter-communal violence which, in its first day, left five people dead and 92 injured (Snider 1968, 965).

The 1969 elections replaced the Alliance, which had ruled the state government in Penang since independence, with Gerakan, an ostensibly non-communal opposition party. In the aftermath of the May 13th riots, the federal government utilized the Internal Security Act to maintain direct control and suspend individual freedoms. Once the parliament was reconvened in 1971, Gerakan elected to join with the Alliance's successor, *Barisan Nasional* (BN). With a firm electoral grip on the state government of Penang and government fears about the strength of the Chinese-based opposition Democratic Action Party (DAP), Gerakan was allowed significant autonomy so long as it (1) did not challenge the system of Malay-preferences established in the NEC and (2) kept ethnic conflict under control.

Gerakan thus faced a severe existential threat. In order to stay in power they had to, on the one hand, maintain the support of the majority Chinese population who demanded an improvement of economic conditions, and on the other, enforce the system of NEP preferences that discriminated against those same Chinese voters.

State resources were highly limited and dependent on the federal government. Since state governments in Malaysia only levy taxes on land, they are highly dependent on the central government providing funding (Narayanan et al. 2009; Hutchinson 2008). But the UMNO-dominated federal government prioritized projects that favored Malay businesses. Figure 4.7 compares federal development allocations per capita between Penang and the rest of Malaysia. Another example of federal antipathy toward Peanang was the government's decision to revoke the state's free-port status in 1969 while promoting Klang Port closer to Kuala Lumpur (Fig. 4.7).

With no natural resources to exploit, a federal government unwilling to expend resources on any programs that targeted Chinese businesses, and a disastrous economic situation, Gerakan had to satisfy its broad coalition by creating developmental institutions.

UMNO at the federal level "could not impose a too Malay-inclined approach in its policies as in the other states primarily because of the fear that its Chinese partners, the Gerakan and MCA, might lose their electoral support to the DAP in the next elections...it has also to ensure that Penang UMNO does not feel a sense of loss, perceived or otherwise, for fear that it might be accused, by Malay radicals within it and in PAS, of conceding too much to the non-Malay BN partners" (Hock 1985, 141).

Veto Players: After the Chinese-dominated but self-described multi-ethnic Gerakan party won a majority in the state elections in 1969, its

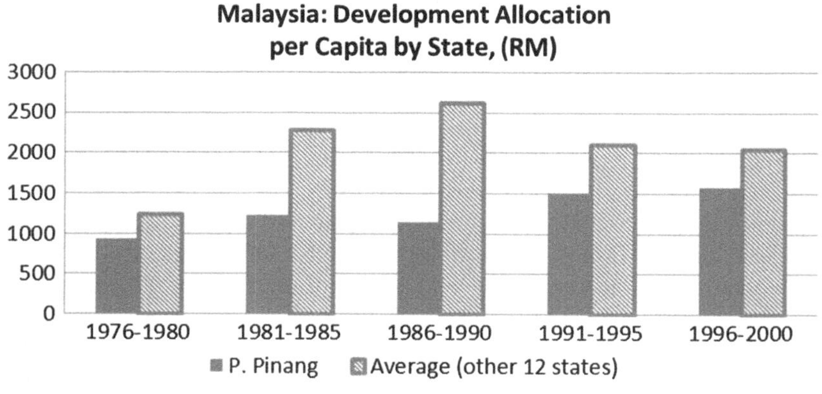

Fig. 4.7 Malaysian federal development expenditures per capita by state

president Lim Chong Eu formed the first state government led by an opposition party. Gerakan joined the Alliance in 1972 and was brought under the BN electoral system with the exception that the MCA and Gerakan openly competed for seats. It retained a high degree of autonomy for Penang. The federal government's commitment to the NEP was paramount but it needed its Chinese partners to maintain harmony and above all keep the opposition DAP out of power. So long as the Gerakan government maintained ethnic harmony and improved conditions for Malays, the center was willing to give the party autonomy. "As a Chinese Chief Minister, Dr Lim has not appeared to be unfair to the Penang Malays in the eyes of federal UMNO despite Penang UMNO's allegations that his measures to help the Penang Malays were halfhearted" (Hock 1985, 146).

But this effort, while successful, was not without cost. "Embarking on economic development meant that the Gerakan had to downplay its political role and concentrate on administration. The latter course of action was bound to create the impression in the more radical sections of the Gerakan's Chinese support that the party had neglected its political principles. Nevertheless the Gerakan leadership was aware that in order to have economic development in the state with funds controlled by a Federal Government whose core policies were different, some political aspirations had to be sacrificed and some electoral support thus lost" (Hock 1985, 138–139). The party's electoral strength declined from 16 out of 27 seats in 1969 to 8 seats in 1982. Though UMNO Penang had the largest portion of seats after 1982, the federal government was worried overt UMNO control of a Chinese-majority state would strengthen the Chinese opposition party, the DAP (Hock 1985).

Thus, state economic policy was determined primarily by one veto player, Gerakan. The state government, facing high vulnerability, was responsible for state fiscal policy and sectoral policy. The federal government (UMNO), facing low vulnerability, determined federal level fiscal and exchange rate policies. So, Penang faced a situation somewhat inverse to that of Thailand in the Semi-Democratic period.

4.3.2 *Policy Environment*

As noted above, the overall Malaysian policy environment was narrowly targeted. However, because UMNO was the vessel for the distribution of these narrowly targeted policies and UMNO was not in direct control of state institutions in Penang, the narrow policy benefits available in other states were less available in Penang. The policy environment in Penang, rather, was determined by the autonomous state government, directed by Gerakan. With a dire economic situation, inter-communal tensions running high, and a federal government willing to suspend democratic niceties looming above, Gerakan needed to deliver growth quickly. With extremely limited revenues, however, they could not spend their way to prosperity. Rather, they combined an effort to court foreign investment while developing domestic industrial capabilities. Though similar to the official policy at the federal level, Penang implemented this strategy without creating a narrowly targeted policy environment.

One of the central instruments of this policy was the Penang Development Corporation (PDC) Established in 1969, the PDC brought together state officials, leading domestic firms, and representatives of multinationals operating in the state. Like the MPHB, PDC was established to facilitate increased professionalism and coordination among firms. Also like the MPHB, the PDC was very closely related to a political party, in this case Gerakan. Gerakan president and Penang Chief Minister, Dr. Lim Chong Eu played a pivotal role in the creation and development of the corporation.

Because the state government's ability to tax was highly constrained, it had to generate revenues by promoting the growth of the state economy as a whole. Using the PDC, it acquired substantial land holdings around the state and converted them into industrial estates (Hutchinson 2008, 227). It then sold some of these holdings at market rates and leased others to companies entering the industrial estates (Warr 1987, 32). Some of these industrial estates served as Malaysia's first free trade zones. The PDC established its first free trade zone in 1972 and was operating four by 1980. The corporation attempted to foster synergies among producers by having them co-locate in industrial estates. It also promoted direct, informal linkages between downstream MNCs and local upstream firms. Additionally, it ensured that MNC and local businesses had a fast-track through federal-level red tape.

The PDC used earnings from these real-estate projects to invest in specific local companies. "By 1980, this totaled some US$6.4 million in seventeen firms…While many of the firms did not turn out to be profitable, these investments served other purposes, such as demonstrating the state government's commitment to a specific sector, reducing risk for local entrepreneurs, and attempting to diversify the economy" (Hutchinson 2008, 227).

The policy environment underwent a significant shift in the early 1980s. The decline in Gerakan's relative power coupled with the overall centralization of power under Mahathir meant that there were new, influence-based points of access to policy-makers. The federal government now had to approve the PDC's investment decisions, audit its finances, appoint politically important representatives to the board (Hutchinson 2008, 229). They also interfered with the state's ability to generate revenue by requisitioning land.

4.3.3 Economic Governance Institutions

As the electronic/electrical industry is the largest and most important manufacturing sector in Penang during this period, I treat the overall assessment of the state's economic governance institutions at the same time as the EEI.

Corporate Governance Institutions: Although the federal rules that apply to firms in Malaysia also apply to firms in Penang, after 1969 Penang's unique policy environment produced different overall patterns of corporate governance. To be sure, firms located in Penang could raise money on the national stock market or with the assistance of patrons in UMNO or the MCA, but the more stable, broadly targeted policy environment created opportunities for coordination in Penang that did not exist in the rest of Malaysia.

Penang's electronics industry began after the state government's push into that sector. The PDC's courtship of large multinational electronics producers brought about a transformation of the state's economy from entrepot in decline to global electronics hub. Integrated circuits, semiconductors, hard disk drives, and other computer components were manufactured by the world's leading MNCs. Local firms sprouted up, expanded, and upgraded to perform original equipment manufacturing, original design manufacturing, and other support services. Table 4.6 shows the distribution of small/medium and large firms in the EEI and photonics sectors in Penang as of 2002.

As in the rest of Malaysia, Small ethnic-Chinese firms remained the most common form of local corporate governance in Penang. But unlike Chinese firms elsewhere, firms in Penang began investing in co-specific assets and hiring professional management.

Table 4.6 Estimated distribution of firm by size in PDC industrial areas

Sector	*Total Factories*	*Small & Medium*	*Percent*	*Large*	*Percent*
Electronics /Electrical	164	76	46.3	88	53.7
Optical Goods, Controlling & Transport Equipment	18	8	44.4	10	55.6
Total	731	524	71.7	207	28.3

Source DCT Consultancy Services Sdn. Bhd., Penang cited in Lee (2006)

> 85% of the local industry in Penang can be classified as SMEs, the majority of which are owned by Chinese. During an interview with representatives from the Chinese Chamber of Commerce in the provincial capital Georgetown it was emphasised that the typical Chinese SME is currently undergoing a change. They are not only family run enterprises but are evolving into more complex and diversified entities, the specific characteristics of which depends on the size and constitution of the individual company. The micro or 'Mom and Pap' Chinese SMEs are typically very small family owned and run companies that produce a rather narrow range of products. This is especially the case if they are suppliers to major local or foreign companies. The small and medium SMEs constitute a more diversified lot. The most efficient of them has hired professional, not necessarily Chinese, managers to run the business in an 'arm's length' mode, but maintain the control over the business strategies themselves. (Jacobsen 2009)

In the EEI sector, firms such as Eng Hardware and LKT Engineering moved beyond the diversified conglomerate structure to become professionally managed, specialized firms.

In 1979, Dato Teh Ah Ba transformed the jig and fixture manufacturing firm, Eng Hardware Electrical, into Eng Hardware Engineering and restructured their operations to provide precision tooling for the growing semiconductor industry in Penang. Eng Hardware particularly benefited from a close working relationship with the representatives of Intel's Penang factories.[8] Using the insights from this experience, they moved into HDD actuator production in 1988 as Penang emerged as a major disk drive manufacturer. The EngTeknology group went public in 1993 with a listing on the Malaysia Securities Exchange but the Teh family retained control. The firm spread operations throughout the electronics industry, using its precision ODM and OEM capabilities to serve the needs of a wide variety of MNCs. As the photonics industry emerged in the early 2000s, the company participated in a forward-looking plan to develop greater skills and capacities (Malaysia Industrial Development Authority 2004, 11). Eng hardware invested heavily in attracting professional, skilled staff and supervisors, with "four engineers, forty qualified technicians and supervisors, and fifty skilled machinists in 1993, compared to none in 1978" (Rasiah 1999, 239).

Like Eng Hardware, Low Kim Teow Engineering (LKT) changed from a small family shophouse to major supplier of precision high technology equipment, high-end automation equipment, and precision engineering services to multinationals operating in Penang by working closely with Intel (Financial Times 1992). Going public in 1995, the company did not diversify into unrelated activities as other successful Chinese conglomerates did in other parts of Malaysia, "We do not intend to diversify into property or construction as yet…Our diversification will involve strengthening our core business and diversify into areas we are very good at…We are going to use the listing exercise as the vehicle for us to go into other areas since currently, we are more on the assembly side…We'd like to go into the testing side as well" (Hamsawi 1995b). Despite the Low family retaining nearly a quarter of total shares, LKT structured its operations using professional management (New Straits Times 2006). "I am not running a Chinaman business. I am running a Malaysian business with our own management style…We don't want to employ relatives to work because in technology, you hire professionals. So our company policy is very simple: Do not hire relatives" (Hamsawi 1995a).

While Penang is better known for firms in the electronics industry, there were also important players in the electrical appliance sector. Keat Radio Co. was created in 1964 by Datuk Chew WengKhak to sell audio visual equipment in Penang. After success in marketing and sales in the Malaysian market, Mr. Chew began manufacturing in 1982 under his own brand, Pensonic. In 1988 they moved on to manufacture electrical appliances under the Pensonic brand. In 1995 the company was listed on the KLSE's second board. During the 1997–1998 crisis, Pensonic made use of state resources to plan its adjustment strategies, including meeting with State Science, Technology and Industrial Transformation Committee chairman Datuk Dr Kang Chin Seng to discuss the possibility of increasing exports (Kathirasen 1998). The company managed to increase the proportion of goods exported from 5% in 1994 to 15% in 2000 (Fatt 2000). In addition to producing under its own brand, Pensonic also offered ODM services to several Japanese and Korean MNCs (Yean 2006). The company made significant use of capital markets to raise money for various operations, but the Chew family always retained a controlling stake.[9] Pensonic also worked closely with a number of local suppliers that emerged in Peanang, including T. H. Hin and Unimech.

T.H.Hin grew up in Penang's industrial estates alongside its local and multinational customers. The company, which listed on the KLSE in 1997, manufactured and distributed electrical household appliances, cast iron products, and spare parts. Producing and selling goods under the brand name Milux, the firm also conducted OEM manufacturing for MNCs like Sanyo, Electrolux, and Whirlpool and for local companies like Pensonic (Ngiam 1997). The company began to diversify into real estate in 2002 but refocused on electrical appliances in 2006.

Unimech, a leading engineering specialist in the "designing, fabrication, installation, testing and commissioning of industrial equipment and plants for steam generation, heating and combustion systems, fluid conveyance piping works, as well as maintenance and overhaul of engineering equipment and equipment part replacing services," was founded in 1977 by Lim CheahChooi and taken public in 2000 (Valve 2010). Outside, professional management was important in the development of the company (Yu 2000). "[Mr. Lim] always believed that there must be key personnel (in place) to manage (parts of) the company…He likes to bring people up, for if you want to be a multi-millionaire, the people beneath you must at least be millionaires"(TejAsia MY Company Annual Reports 2002). Later that year, Unimech moved upstream, acquiring a manufacturer of coatings materials, chemical products and cementitious products to complement its industrial manufacturing operations (Bernama Daily Malaysian News 2002). But Unimech remained focused on their core EEI business(Tan 2007). They then began expanding labor-intensive manufacturing operations to other Southeast Asian countries and China.

This shift to professionally managed but family-controlled firms indicates the development of more coordinative economic governance institutions in this period.

Inter-firm Relations: Inter-firm relations were highly coordinative in Penang. Local firms and MNCs worked together and shared critical information about their operations regularly through networks at various stages of institutionalization.

The PDC played matchmaker between MNCs looking for suppliers and local firms open to expansion and upgrading. This matchmaking went far beyond facilitating arms-length transactions between customer and supplier. The resulting vertical partnerships led to additional funding resources to the local suppliers in order to facilitate the upgrading of their production capabilities. Thus it was that Intel Penang was able to form partnerships with Eng Hardware, Loh Kim Teow, Prodelcon, and Metfab; Motorola formed links with Actacorp, TAC Precision, and Wong Engineering; and Sharp Roxy with Atlan Industries. These local partners were not made dependent suppliers, but were helped to develop genuine upgrading such that many were able to produce for and sell to other MNCs in the industry.

Actors across and throughout the state were willing to invest in these co-specific assets. The MNCs spent substantial time and resources facilitating the development of local capacities, trusting that the partners would be able to deliver in the long-term; local firms invested in the technologies and processes required by their foreign partners, trusting that the future orders would come. Though these relationships were mostly interpersonal and not formalized or institutionalized, the local chambers of commerce also participated in the linkage formation process led by the PDC (Rasiah 2003, 17).

MNCs and local firms took full advantage of their co-location in the same industrial zones. This helped strengthen links. "During the 1970s and early 1980s, managers from the Bayan Lepas FTZ would meet at the restaurant of the nearby international airport for lunch or after work, a role which was later assumed by the Equatorial Hotel. Several managers reported that such informal meetings facilitated information exchange on such issues as labor recruitment problems and capacity sub-contracting" (Felker 1998b, 355).

In the early 1990s, the government sought to formalize the personal relationships that had developed in the previous decades, creating Human-Resources Development Council (HRDC) and the Penang Industrial Council, but these efforts were not as successful as the partnerships of the earlier period.

Inter-firm linkage institutions were coordinated in this period with significant sharing of information among firms and high levels of co-specific assets.

4.4 Conclusion

Between independence and 2006, Malaysia experienced three different configurations of structural and institutional factors. The table highlights the number of veto players, the degree of vulnerability, the expected policy environment, and the observed policy environment for each observation.

From 1957 to 1969, the federal government was governed by one veto player and faced moderate vulnerability. The model used in this dissertation leads us to expect that the policy environment should be stable and a mix of narrowly and broadly targeted policies. The observed policy environment was stable but predominantly broadly targeted. Government infrastructure and development projects were largely confined to the agricultural and extractive sectors.

After the riots of 1969 the structural and institutional conditions in the state of Penang and the rest of the country diverged. For the federal government and most of the country, increasing resource revenues enabled the now single veto player government to overcome increased sensitivity to unrest by distributing narrowly targeted policy benefits. As expected the policy environment was unpredictable and narrowly targeted in this period.

In Penang however, the Gerakan party maintained significant autonomy and shared power with the UMNO-dominated federal government. With an extremely dire economic situation, ethnic tensions running high, and no hope of meaningful economic support from the federal government, the state government could not afford to distribute narrowly-targeted side payments. Rather, as predicted, they maintained a stable, broadly-targeted policy environment.

From 1957 to 1969 the policy environment created by the federal government was stable but predominantly broadly targeted. The model used by this dissertation suggests that we should observe coordinated economic governance institutions in this period. In fact, we see the growth of both liberal and hierarchical institutions in both corporate governance and inter-firm linkage institutions.

After 1969, the federal-level policy environment was unpredictable and particularistic. The model indicates that we should expect an increase in hierarchical governance institutions in this period. This was observed in both corporate governance and inter-firm linkage institutions. Most successful firms were controlled by either families or UMNO clients.

The state of Penang featured a stable, broadly-targeted policy environment. We should thus expect to see the development of coordinative governance institutions. Penang indeed developed strong inter-firm linkage institutions that facilitated information sharing and co-specific assets. With regard to corporate governance, successful firms remained predominantly family-owned but many developed professional management and skill-provision systems.

Notes

1. In 1955 the MCA were able to prevent the adoption of proposed special rights for Malays that in many ways went further than the eventual NEP (Heng 1998, 60). After UMNO Minister of Agriculture and Cooperatives, Abdul Aziz bin Ishak, revoked the licenses of several hundred Chinese rice millers in the early 1960s, the MCA was able to pressure the government into dismissing Aziz from the cabinet and backing down from the seizure of Chinese mills by threatening to withdraw from the coalition (Bowie 1991, 74–75).
2. This process was not without controversy. In 1954 UMNO refused the demands of MCA president Lim Chong Eu to expand the number of seats that the MCA contested from 31 to 40 (Heng 1998), leading to the end of Lim's reign as party head.
3. The shock caused by British devaluation of the Pound in 1967 did present a problem for authorities as the value of old currency notes, still in wide circulation, was tied to the pound while newer notes were backed directly by gold (Snider 1968, 963–964). But as this was an external shock it is not evidence of either policy volatility or a narrowly targeted policy.
4. Slater describes the resulting 'protection-pact' in greater detail. "Ordering Power: Contentious Politics, State-Building, and Authoritarian Durability in Southeast Asia," 279–280, 304.
5. There was a 152% increase in the combined value of petroleum, tin, rubber, palm oil, and natural gas between 1976 and 1980—see Fig. 4.2.
6. It should be noted that this was not an entirely seamless transition. UMNO itself was nearly ripped apart by the conflict between the bureaucrats that had benefited under the SOE system and the new Malay industrialists that wanted to divvy up the state resources. For more on this, see Syn (2002).
7. More in the next chapter.
8. More in the next Section.
9. In 1998, Neico Industries (formerly Sanyo Industries Malaysia) bought a 10% stake in Pensonic (Reuters News 1998).

References

Andaya, B. W., & Andaya, L. Y. (2001). *A history of Malaysia*. Honolulu, HI: University of Hawaii Press.

Bernama Daily Malaysian News. (2002). Adopt "X-Plus One" formula to stay competitive, Says Koh.

Bernama Infolink Services. (1999). Malaysian factfiles—Industries and industrial development—Malaysia Electric Corporation (MEC)—Mec City.

Bisnis Indonesia. (2006). Daikin Officially Acquires OYL.
Bowie, A. (1991). *Crossing the Industrial Divide: State, Society, and the Politics of Economic Transformation in Malaysia*. New York: Columbia University Press.
Brown, G K. (2005). Playing the (Non) Ethnic Card: The Electoral System and Ethnic Voting Patterns in Malaysia. *Ethnopolitics*, Routledge *4*(4), 429–445.
Burton, J. (2004, January 20). Businessmen feel the winds of change as Malaysia moves to end "crony capitalism": New Prime Minister Abdullah Badawi aims to stamp out the informal lobbying of officials for contracts. *Financial Times*.
Case, W. (2008). Malaysia in 2007: High corruption and low opposition. *Asian Survey, 48*(1), 47–54.
Chin, J. (2010). Malaysia: The rise of Najib and 1Malaysia. *Southeast Asian Affairs, 2010*(1), 164–179.
Fatt, L. K. (2000). Pensonic all set to go worldwide. *The New Straits Times*.
Felker, G. (1998a). Malaysia's industrial technology development: Firms, policies, and political economy. *Industrial technology development in Malaysia: Industry and firm studies*. New York: Routledge.
Felker, G. (1998b). *Upwardly global? The state, business, and MNCS in Malaysia and Thailand's technological transformation*. Princeton, NJ: Princeton University.
Financial Times. (1992). Supplier to the Multinationals.
Giroud, A. (2003). *Transnational corporations, technology and economic development: Backward linkages and knowledge transfer in South-East Asia*. Gloucestershire: Edward.
Gomez, E. T. (2002). *Political business in East Asia*. Oxfordshire: Routledge.
Gomez, E. T. (2008). Enterprise development and inter-ethnic relations in Malaysia. In R. S. K. Wong (Ed.), *Chinese entrepreneurship in a global era* (p. 91). Boca Raton, FL: Taylor & Francis.
Gomez, E. T. (2009). The rise and fall of capital: Corporate Malaysia in historical perspective. *Journal of Contemporary Asia, 39*(3), 345–381.
Hai, L. H. (2002). Electoral politics in Malaysia: "Managing" elections in a plural society. In A. Croissant (Ed.), *Electoral politics in Southeast & East Asia*. Friedrich Ebert Stiftung: Singapore.
Hamid, H. (1995). Govt aims to increase anchor companies in vendor scheme. *Business Times (Malaysia)*.
Hamsawi, R. (1995a). LKT Ind sees rise in pre-tax turnover. *Business Times (Singapore)*.
Hamsawi, R. (1995b). Loh's ambitious dream come true. *Business Times (Malaysia)*.
Heng, P. K. (1998). Chinese responses to Malay hegemony in Peninsular Malaysia (1957–1996). In *cultural contestations: Mediating identities in a changing malaysian society* (pp. 51–83). London: ASEA Academic Press.

Hicken, A. (2007). Omitted variables, intent, and counterfactuals: A response to Michael H. Nelson. *Journal of East Asian Studies, 7*, 149–158.

Hightower, S. (1994). Air quality control products maker sold to Malaysian group. *The Associated Press.*

Hock, C. H. (1985). Some observations on coalition politics in Penang. *Modern Asian Studies, 19*(1), 125–146.

Hutchinson, F. E. (2008). "Developmental" states and economic growth at the sub-national level. *Southeast Asian Affairs*, 223–244.

Jacobs, J. (1993). Local participation in electronics industry wanting. *Business Times (Malaysia).*

Jacobsen, M. (2009). Frozen identities. Inter-ethnic relations and economic development in Penang, Malaysia. In *Asia Research Centre* (Vol. 30).

Jesudason, J. V. (1989). *Ethnicity and the economy: the state, Chinese business, and multinationals in Malaysia. Ethnicity and the economy: The state, Chinese business, and multinationals in Malaysia.* New York: Oxford University Press.

Johnson, S. (2006). *Malaysian capital controls: Macroeconomics and Institutions.* Washington, D.C.: International Monetary Fund.

Johnson, S., & Mitton, T. (2003). Cronyism and capital controls: Evidence from Malaysia. *Journal of Financial Economics, 67*(2), 351–382.

Jomo, K. S., & Gomez, E. T. (2000). The Malaysian development dilemma. In M. H. Khan & J. K. Sundaram (Eds.), *Rents, rent-seeking and economic development: Theory and evidence in Asia* (pp. 274–303). Cambridge: Cambridge University Press.

K'Zaman, B. (1994). MEEIG plea against protection withdrawl. *Business Times (Malaysia).*

Kathirasen, A. (1998). Pensonic optimistic of RM120 m turnover. *The New Straits Times.*

Kaufmann, D., Kraay, A., & Mastruzzi, M. (2012). The worldwide governance indicators, 2011 Update, Aggregate indicators of governance 1996–2010. Downloaded May.

Kenney, M., Han, K., & Tanaka, S. (2002). Scattering geese: The venture capital industries of East Asia: A report to the World Bank.

Lee, H K. (2006). *Enhancing Global Competitiveness of Penang Electronics and Electrical Small and Medium Industries through Improving Linkage Programmes.* Ph.D. thesis, Universiti Teknologi Malaysia.

Lopez, L. (2004, September 27). Abdullah dealt setback in Malaysia party polls—Allies' unexpected losses may hurt premier's plan to weed out corruption. *The Asian Wall Street Journal.*

MacIntyre, A. (2003a). Institutions and investors: The politics of the economic crisis in Southeast Asia. *International Organization, 55*(1), 81–122.

MacIntyre, A. (2003b). *The power of institutions: Political architecture and governance.* Ithaca: Cornell University Press.

Malaysia Industrial Development Authority. (2004). Photonics: Opportunities for growth in Malaysia.
Martin, D. (2012, July 1). Sensational Malaysian submarine scandal resurfaces. *Agence France Presse.*
Narayanan, S. (1996). Fiscal reform in Malaysia: Behind a successful experience. *Asian Survey, 36*(9), 869–881.
Narayanan, S., Hui, L. M., & Leng, O. W. (2009). Re-examining state finances and governance: The challenge for Penang. In *PENANG OUTLOOK Forum.* Socio-Economic & Environmental Research Institute.
New Straits Times. (1997). MEC invites SMIs to join programme.
New Straits Times. (2006). LKT industrial berhad—Malaysia company factfile.
New Straits Times. (2007). Personality profile: Omar Ong Yoke Lin, Tun.
Ngiam, D. (1997). T.H. Hin to increase high-end mart exports. *The New Straits Times.*
Nurani, N. (2001). The business that Shamsuddin built. *Malaysian Business (New Straits Times).*
Pak, S. (1991). Restructured KLI grabs limelight on its re-listing. *The Straits Times.*
Ping, L. P., & Yean, T. S. (2007). Malaysia ten years after the Asian financial crisis. *Asian Survey, 47*(6), 915–929.
Rasiah, R. (1999). Government-business co-ordination and the development of eng hardware. *Industrial technology development in Malaysia: Industry and firm studies.* Oxfordshire: Routledge.
Rasiah, R. (2003). *Fostering clusters in the Malaysian electronics industry.*
Rasiah, R., & Shari, I. (2001). Market, government and Malaysia's new economic policy. *Cambridge Journal of Economics, 25*(1), 57.
Reuters News. (1998). Neico buys 10 pct of Pensonic.
Rudner, M. (1994). *Malaysian development: A retrospective.* Ottawa: Carleton University Press.
Searle, P. (1998). *The riddle of Malaysian capitalism: Rent-seekers or real capitalists?* Sydney: Allen & Unwin.
Select Federal Filings Newswires. (1995). AAF-McQuay Inc.: Company background/capitalization. Dow Jones & Company, Inc.
Sheng, A. (1989). Bank restructuring in Malaysia: 1985–1988. *The World Bank: Policy Research Working Paper Series.*
Singh, B. (2009). Malaysia in 2008: The elections that broke the tiger's back. *Asian Survey, 49*(1), 156–165.
Slater, D. (2005). *Ordering power: Contentious politics, state-building, and authoritarian durability in Southeast Asia.* Atlanta: Emory University.
Snider, N. L. (1968). What happened in Penang? *Asian Survey, 8*(12), 960–975.
Sutter, J. O. (1966). Two faces of Konfrontasi: Crush Malaysia and the Gestapu. *Asian Survey, 6*(10), 523–546.

Syn, T. W. (2002). Privatisation and capital accumulation in Malaysia. In *University of Manchester, Institute for Development Policy and Management (IDPM)*. Centre on Regulation and Competition (CRC) Working papers.

Tahir, Z. (1996). Take in more firms under vendor scheme. *Business Times (Malaysia)*.

Tan, D. (2007). Electronics to drive Unimech. *Star Business*.

TejAsia MY Company Annual Reports. (2002, February). Atlan Holdings Berhad.

The New Straits Times. (1996). KLIG buying into Australian firm.

Thoburn, J. (1978). Malaysia's tin supply problems. *Resources Policy, 4*(1), 31–34.

UN Comtrade. (2012). *United Nations*.

Valve, A. (2010). UNIMECH Group Berhad.

Lam, Van. (1978). Incidence of tin export taxation in West Malaysia. *The Developing Economies, 16*(4), 434–445.

Warr, P. G. (1987). Malaysia's industrial enclaves: Benefits and costs. *The Developing Economies, 25*(1), 30–55.

World Corruption Barometer. (2012). *Transparency International*.

Yean, N. K. (2006). Corporate: Pensonic finds footing in tough business. *The Edge Financial Daily*.

Young, K., Bussink, W. C. F., & Hasan, P. (1980). *malaysia, growth and equity in a multiracial society*. Published for the World Bank [by] Johns Hopkins University Press.

Yu, L. C. (2000). Going for listing: Unimech aims for higher exports. *The Edge Weekly Provider*.

CHAPTER 5

Singapore: Constraints and Coordination

5.1 Constraints

Systemic Vulnerability: Singapore became an independent state in 1965, after a period of increasing self-rule under the British and a brief union with Malaysia. The new country faced threats on many fronts. As an island-state with a majority Chinese population surrounded by much larger ethnically Malay states, Singapore was especially vulnerable to military attack. It faced serious internal threats from both inter-communal and class conflict that threatened to bring about foreign intervention. Without any meaningful natural resources, the state was highly vulnerable.

With a very tenuous handle on its own inter-ethnic situation, Malaysia was very wary of Singapore with its majority Chinese population. The ruling PAP's vision of a strongly multi-ethnic nation clashed with UMNO's strategy for managing race relations. Indeed, this was one of the chief reasons Singapore had been ejected from the federation. With an active branch of UMNO in Singapore and the Malaysian government keeping a watchful eye on the PAP's treatment of Malays, relations were highly strained (Chang 1968, 766). To make matters worse, Singapore was dependent on Malaysia for over half its water in those early years and its main forts were always within range of Malaysian artillery (Matthews and Yan 2007). The threat of invasion from the much larger, more populous country was real.

J.D. Moore, *Varieties of Capitalism in Southeast Asia*, The Political Economy of East Asia, DOI 10.1007/978-3-319-53700-9_5

Meanwhile, the even more populous Indonesia was a potential threat as well. The Malay-speaking country had open, low-level conflict with Britain and Malaysia (which included Singapore at the time) in the form of Konfrontasi from 1962 to 1966. Though relations improved under General Suharto, the size discrepancy made the Singaporean government concerned about even a small chance for conflict.

PM Lee Kuan Yew made the government's perception of this vulnerability clear:

> We want peace simply because we have not the capacity to make war on anybody. We are surrounded by bigger and more powerful neighbors with whom we cannot afford to settle disputes by force of arms. My country is well aware that it is situated in a region of the world which has traditionally been the battleground of big power conflict. Singapore itself, by virtue of its location, has attracted the attention of nations who wish to dominate Southeast Asia. -*The New Straits Times*, quoted in Chang (1968, 766).

The Singaporean government has been very concerned about mass unrest since independence. After WWII various labor groups and leftist organizations became important political forces. Many of these groups were strongly pro-communist (some with ties to the Malayan Communist Party) and strikes were frequent and often violent (Bradley 1965, 293). The country lost over a million man-days of labor between April 1946 and March 1947 alone. "Virtually every type of worker in Singapore was involved in a strike at some stage of the year and many were involved in more than one" (Giap 1976, 105). The power of unions to mobilize a highly discontented population meant an increased threat of interference by communist China on the one hand and conservative Malaysia and Great Britain on the other.

Lee Kuan Yew's PAP emerged and thrived in this period of great tumult, relying especially on labor groups for support (Lian 1969). Lee and the PAP moderates eventually isolated the party's extreme-left wing over the issue of unification with Malaysia. But after separation from the federation, the continued survival of the new state required that the government ensure the acquiescence of other labor and communal groups. Continued unrest would threaten the economic and political stability of the new country and if Malaysia or other powers in the region thought the new island state might become a hotbed of communist activity, its continued existence could be in jeopardy.

The labor movement was split into the Singapore Association of Trade Unions (SATU), alleged to be linked with the Malayan Communist party and associated with the left-wing faction of the PAP and the Singapore National Trade Union Congress, associated with Lee Kuan Yew's moderate faction. By the time of independence, Lee's success at routing the left-leaning faction of PAP had greatly undermined the SATU (Luther 1979). The government further used the coercive capacities enshrined in the Internal Security Act to target the existing labor organizational structure. At the same time, it strengthened and supported the hierarchically structured National Trade Union Congress to circumvent the Singapore Association of Trade Unions (Mauzy and Milne 2002). Though this reduced the influence of the movement's more activist leaders, continued quiescence would require declines in unemployment and wage improvements.

As mentioned above, race relations were tense at independence and any inter-ethnic violence threatened relations with neighboring Malaysia. The depth of the threat was demonstrated when widespread, week-long rioting erupted in July of 1964, leaving 35 dead and over 500 injured. The protests that triggered the violence were allegedly instigated by extremist Malays in Singapore's UMNO chapter (Leifer 1964). Chinese middle schools, secret societies, and labor and business associations had also protested frequently in Singapore's formative years (Carnell 1955). Ensuring that Chinese, Malay, and Indian groups had a stake in the new government thus became a major priority.

Singapore had virtually no easily exploitable resources to finance either its military or coalitional needs. What little balance had been achieved by independence was undermined by the removal of the British military presence in 1968. The withdrawal had a devastating impact on the Singaporean economy, leading to the loss of 40,000 jobs and a fifth of Singapore's national income (Matthews and Yan 2007).

By the early 1970s, unemployment had declined significantly with the influx of FDI. But Singapore's dependence on foreign multinationals placed it in a precarious position, dependent on the whims of international capital and global market forces. So long as it was competing based on low wages, there was no guarantee that the economic hardships and resulting social strife of earlier periods could not return and threaten the continued existence of the state.

With the threat of mass unrest on multiple fronts with the real potential of bringing about an armed conflict with one of Singapore's much larger neighbors, the pressure to, on the one hand, deliver side payments to a broad section of society and, on the other, quickly and drastically increase the size of its military were immense. With no easily extractable resources, however, the government had to develop strong growth-inducing institutions by limiting corruption and ensuring a stable policy environment.

Veto Players: Since independence, Singapore has had a single political party dominate the political landscape. Two major factions competed for control of the PAP in the period of increasing self-rule under the British: Lee's moderates and the leftists. After splitting from the PAP in 1961, the leftists formed Barisan Socialis and were promptly buried in the push for merger with Malaya (Mauzy and Milne 2002).

With uncontested control of the legislature and armed with a powerful set of internal security laws, the PAP has acted as an uncontested, single veto player since independence. While considerable discretion was given to bureaucrats to implement and enforce PAP policy, party officials remained in control (Mauzy and Milne 2002).

This framework suggests that a single veto player constrained by the demands of high levels of systemic vulnerability should have a stable, broadly targeted policy environment that results in coordinative economic governance institutions.

5.2 Policy Environment

The economic policy environment was broadly targeted and stable in this period. Macroeconomic policy stability was a primary goal for the PAP. As a small country, that was highly dependent on international trade, Singapore was highly vulnerable to global market fluctuations. Oil shocks and global recessions had the potential to greatly disrupt the city-state's economy. As such, the government's interventions were well beyond the typical macroeconomic policy levers typically employed. In addition to a strictly balanced budget and the careful use of a currency board to further insulate the small economy, the government also used labor market regulations and the promotion of high savings rates. Because the government maintained tight controls on wages and unions, it was able to reserve exchange rate manipulations for combating inflation (Huff 1995).

Ensuring high savings was another key way in which the government ensured a stable macroeconomic environment. In 1963 Singapore's economic architect, Goh Keng Swee, argued that, "the paramount need…in an economy which wants to expand its basic wealth at a fast rate, a target like 20% or more should be aimed at" (Singapore Legislative Assembly, November 1963, cited in Huff 1995, 1426). From very low levels at independence, Singapore became the world's top saver by 1980.

With relatively constant public spending as a share of GDP, much of the savings increase came from forced private savings (Huff 1995, 1999). The state "used the monopoly power of statutory boards to extract an 'economic surplus' from consumers…Implicit taxation of consumers effectively mobilized savings" (Huff 1995, 1427). A large portion of this came from the Central Provident Fund, a social security scheme. "the Central Provident Fund's effect was to raise Singapore's overall savings rate by 3.8% during 1967–1989" (Monetary Authority of Singapore, 1991 cited in Huff 1995, 1428). But because much of these savings were invested abroad, rather than in Singapore, most of the investments that did occur were privately directed and free from the sorts of patronage-directed investments that were common in Malaysia NEP. This outflow of funds also helped maintain macroeconomic stability by offsetting FDI in the current account.

After a recession in the mid-1980s, the Singaporean government sought to intervene in the economy, promoting higher value-added sectors and small- and medium-sized enterprises. Institutions were created to ensure that wages, already too high to ensure continued competitiveness in labor-intensive industries, kept pace with productivity improvements. Additionally, the government tried to foster faster technological advance among local SMEs (Trocki 2006, 159–157). Great care was taken to ensure that those bureaucrats which had discretion in sectoral policy implementation would not use their influence for personal gain. The PAP created and backed powerful anti-corruption institutions to monitor powerful government officials (Schein 1996, 172). Additionally, the government provided above-market compensation to officials to reduce the temptation to derive financial benefits from office (Bellows 2009, 35–38).

Since independence, the PAP has formulated and employed policies that followed a stable set of policy objectives.

5.3 Economic Governance Institutions

In Singapore, as in Penang, the EEI industry has been the most important manufacturing sector. As such, EEI economic governance institutions will be analyzed concurrently with the overall characterization of the economy.

Corporate Governance: The Singaporean economy has been dominated by multinational corporations and government-linked corporations (GLC). Among non-governmental, local companies, the family firm has been the primary form of corporate governance. Like Thailand, Malaysia, and many other countries in East and Southeast Asia, Singapore's family firms had traditionally been diversified conglomerates that relied on family for management and capital. Over time, however, these firms increasingly grew to rely on non-family members for critical managerial tasks and rely on venture capital and alternative sources of finance.

Despite a long tradition of British capital markets under colonial rule, Singaporean firms and investors were wary of liberal-style diffuse shareholding arrangements. Lee Kuan Yew noted:

> The old family business in Singapore is one of the problems in Singapore…business is kept in the family. And the idea of sinking money into an anonymous corporation run by professionals over whom they have no direct personal control is foreign to them … So we have to accelerate this process. (Kwang et al. 2015, 187)

Despite the strong preference of families to retain control of their companies, many opted to bring on non-family management. In a survey of Chinese family businesses in Singapore, Tsui-Auch found a marked shift to professional, non-family management even where the businesses continued to be 'ruled' by the families.[1] This transition was not due mostly to dynastic succession within families. Of the 19 sampled companies that made the transition to non-family management in the 1970s and 1980s, 15 were still owned by first generation founders (Tsui-Auch 2004).

As with the economy more generally, corporate governance in the EEI sector was a mix of hierarchical and coordinative corporate governance institutions. The family firm remained the predominant form of corporation, but they tended to focus on the IIE sector and made use of professional management outside of the firm.

Microfits and Methods was established as an engineering company to supply tooling parts to multinationals in Singapore in 1978 by Jimmy Chew, an engineer at Fairchild, and three partners. They moved from a single contract with Japanese semiconductor producer, NEC, to contracts with several US multinationals. In the mid-1980s, with financial assistance from the Economic Development Board (EDB) and corporate investor Lim Teck Lee, the company, now called Advanced Systems

Automation (ASA), was "given responsibility for developing new, specialist semiconductor encapsulation molding machines" (Mathews 1999, 19). ASA proceeded to form joint ventures with several multinational companies in the semiconductor industry. In 1989, US-based venture capital firm Hambrecht and Quist invested S$1.6 million in Microfits and Methods to facilitate a new JV with Labinal (Cua 1989). Before they had offered IPO on the Sesdaq in 1996, the company was owned by several players. Founders Jimmy Chew and Kwok Choong Whye held 20%, the Economic Development Board held 17%, Hambrecht and Quist held 17%, and the Lim Teck Lee trading group held 45% (Rajendran 1994). In the late 1990s, after listing, the founders' shareholdings were further diluted well below the 10% mark, leaving ASA a highly successful widely held Singaporean corporation.

Manufacturing Integration Technology (MIT) was established by Tony Kwong, an engineer, in 1989. In 1992 the company became incorporated under the MIT name. The company designs, develops, manufactures, and distributes automated equipment for the semiconductor industry. The company grew "to become one of the most significant of Singapore 'Enterprise 50' firms, expanding its operations into Europe, North America and Asia" (Mathews 1999). They received a S$1.5 million grant from the EDB in 1996 to implement the 'Fully Automated EOL Process'. The EDB also took a 15% stake in the company, providing professional advice and helping to secure grants (Chew 1999). MIT went public in 1999, diluting the Kwon family's stake to 54.9% and the EDB's to 11.2% (Chan 1999). The EDB completely divested its shares in 2006. Though Chew retained a controlling stake in the firm, he made attracting professional, highly skilled workers and management a top priority (Teik 2000).

Other highly successful Singaporean IIE-focused firms that relied on family ownership but professional management included International Semiconductor Products, SingaTrust, and MBE Technology Pte (Straits Times 1997).

While the ideal-type 'Chinese family firm' utilized family members and personal networks to attract capital, Singaporean firms increasingly used local and foreign venture capital and the stock market to fund business activities. Though such practices are common in liberal market economies, venture funds in Singapore operated more like institutional investors in coordinated market economies.

> Relationships and knowledge of the applicant are also important in the West. But it is possible for individuals to 'walk in the door' and receive funding. In Singapore such applications for funding can occur but in practice are far less likely to attract funding. Cultural-cognitive factors often create the requirement for existing relationships, in order for firms to achieve funding...The venture capitalists interviewed generally agreed that this was one facet of their work that they did not expect to change soon, although the government was encouraging them to be less conservative in providing funding. Once a firm is selected for funding, the venture capitalist will closely monitor the investment. In the West, such monitoring typically occurs through board membership for the venture capitalist. Additionally, the venture capitalist will interact extensively with the funded firm...venture capitalists interviewed generally indicated that they continued to rely on connections and relationships with the funded firm to aid in the monitoring process. These provided venture capitalists with access to senior management and other important individuals, and with more reliable and timely information than they could otherwise have enjoyed. These relationships are also likely to be particularly useful for access to non-codified information, which may be particularly important in early stage monitoring. (Bruton et al. 2002, 209–210)

Venture capital funds based investments and lending on relationships and reputations to a greater degree than outside of Singapore and monitored firms more closely, sometimes using private, non-market information gathered directly from firms themselves. Although, as indicated above, Singaporean family firms are more coordinative than their Thai and Malaysian counterparts, the predominance of family firms is greater than predicted by this framework.[2]

Inter-firm Linkage Institutions: Inter-firm linkage institutions have been highly coordinative in Singapore. Both local and multinational firms have demonstrated a willingness to invest in co-specific assets and share information.

After the recession of the mid-1980s, the Singaporean government sought to facilitate the development of local capital. It launched the Good Manufacturing Practice scheme and the Local Industrial Upgrading Programme (LUIP) to foster long-term supply contracts with multinationals operating in Singapore. Unlike the subsequent Vendor Development program in Malaysia and the BUILD program in Thailand but like the PDC's linkage promotion efforts in Penang, multinationals in Singapore were "willing to send their managers to train local suppliers because they would eventually benefit from their improvement in product quality" (Tsui-Auch 2003, 208).

The programs "provided benefits to small firms in selected local industries, including the semiconductor cluster. MNEs [multinational enterprises] were encouraged to enter into long-term supply contracts with such firms, upgrading their quality and reliability, and technological levels, in the process. Small firms supplying maintenance services, components and equipment to the semiconductor MNEs particularly benefited by this new approach" (Mathews 1999, 19). Thus, local companies were willing to acquire co-specific assets, whose value depended on suppliers and customers. Foreign multinational corporations played a critical role in this effort.

> By the mid-1990s there were 32 MNEs enrolled in the LIUP...Many of the semiconductor multinationals saw it as being in their direct interests to have local Singaporean vendors/suppliers whose quality and delivery could be relied upon, and so they participated in the LIUP. One of these was SGS-Thomson. It has been instrumental in helping a number of small local firms to upgrade their operations, such as by taking delegations to Europe, and introducing the Singapore firms to suppliers there. In some cases this leads to joint ventures being established between the two – enhancing their own capabilities, and making life a little easier for SGS-Thomson globally (in having one superior supplier in place of two). Other multinationals, like Intel or Siemens (a major customer of MIT) enforce upgrading their imposing their own qualifying standards on suppliers. (Mathews 1999, 20–21)[3]

Inter-firm linkage institutions in Singapore often featured the sharing of critical information between local firms, multinationals, and GLCs. Several research consortia were established in Singapore. Unlike similar institutions in Malaysia and Thailand, these featured substantial participation by participating private companies. The Institute of Microelectronics (IME) was established in 1991 with the National University of Singapore and the National Science and Technology Board. IME engages in research and development with individual firms and with groups of firms. "In 1995...a group of companies joined with the IME to form a consortium to improve packaging technologies such as ball grid array; the project focuses on core technological characteristics such as enhanced electrical performance and miniaturization technologies which will then be available to all 12 participants...In this way, the IME acts as "broker" in bringing together companies with advanced skills, to ensure that these are diffused and extended" (Mathews 1999, 22). Other examples of intensive inter-firm linkage coordination include the development of memory chip fabrication and several wafer fabrication parks.

As expected, the corporate governance and inter-firm linkage institutions were highly coordinative in Singapore. Foreign and local firms were willing to make investments in time, information, and capital whose payoff would depend on the active participation of other actors over whom they had no control.

5.4 Conclusion

Singapore has faced high levels of systemic vulnerability since independence. It had no easily exploitable resources with which to keep intercommunal and labor tensions under control. Additionally, there was a real threat that regional powers would intervene if these tensions ever resulted in widespread civil strife. In order to afford both high military expenditures and the provision of side-payments sufficient to keep the population quiescent, the single veto player PAP government had to grow the economy. This required strict limits on particularism and policy volatility. The resulting broadly targeted, stable policy environment facilitated the development of coordinative corporate governance and inter-firm linkage institutions. As in Penang, Chinese family firms retained ownership of their firms but hired professional management and did not diversify out of core industries.

Notes

1. Tsui-Auch defined "those who occupy top management positions or who hold strategic decision-making power as the ones who exercise corporate rule, and those who occupy middle or lower management positions or who run the day-to-day operations as the ones who manage" Tsui-Auch (2004).
2. This may be simply due to the pace of institutional change. Singapore's economy has changed dramatically within a generation. It may be that the current professionally managed family firm is a transitional institution and will gradually give way to widely held corporations over time. This possibility is considered in greater detail in the conclusion of this book. While it is certainly too early to know whether this is a transitory institutional

form or a unique style of corporate governance, with the rapid rise of the People's Republic of China's economy.

3. The behavior of MNCs in Penang and Singapore suggests that the received wisdom regarding their unwillingness to share technological know-how to local firms is not the whole story. I consider the implications of their relationship with local companies in the conclusion.

References

Bellows, T. (2009). Meritocracy and the Singapore political system. *Asian Journal of Political Science, 17*(1), 24–44.

Bradley, C. P. (1965). Leftist fissures in Singapore politics. *The Western Political Quarterly, 18*(2), 292–308.

Bruton, G. D., Ahlstrom, D., & Singh, K. (2002). The Impact of the institutional environment on the venture capital industry in Singapore. *Venture Capital, 4*(3), 197–218.

Carnell, F. G. (1955). Political ferment in Singapore. *Far Eastern Survey, 24*(7), 97–102.

Chan, D. (1999). MIT prices shares at 56 Cents. *Straits Times.*

Chang, D. W. (1968). Nation-building in Singapore. *Asian Survey, 8*(9), 761–773.

Chew, M. (1999). MIT expected to launch mainboard IPO next week. *Business Times (Singapore).*

Cua, G. (1989). US venture capital firm invests in two local names. *Business Times (Singapore).*

Giap, T. S. (1976). Industrial conflict in Malaya, prelude to the communist revolt of 1948. *T'oung Pao.* JSTOR.

Huff, W. G. (1995). The developmental state, government, and Singapore's economic development since 1960. *World Development, 23*(8), 1421–1438.

Huff, W G. (1999). "Singapore's Economic Development: Four Lessons and Some Doubts". *Oxford Development Studies, 27*(1), Routledge, 33–55.

Kwang, H. F., Fernandez, W., & Tan, S. (2015). *Lee Kuan Yew: the man and his ideas.* Marshall Cavendish International Asia Pte Ltd. Chicago.

Leifer, M. (1964). Communal violence in Singapore. *Asian Survey, 4*(10), 1115–1121.

Lian, P. C. (1969). The People's Action Party, 1954–1963. *Journal of Southeast Asian History, 10*(1), 142–154.

Luther, H. (1979). The repression of labour protest in Singapore: Unique case or future model? *Development and Change, 10*(2), 287–299.

Mathews, J. A. (1999). A Silicon island of the east: Creating a semiconductor industry in Singapore. *California Management Review, 41,* 55–78.

Matthews, R., & Yan, N. Z. (2007). Small country "total defence": A case study of Singapore. *Defence Studies, 7*(3), 376–395.

Mauzy, D. K., & Milne, R. S. (2002). *Singapore politics under the People's Action Party*. Routledge: Politics in Asia series. London.
Rajendran, J. (1994). Advanced system automation plans new products, markets. *Business Times (Singapore)*.
Schein, E. H. (1996). *Strategic pragmatism: The culture of Singapore's Economic Development Board*. Cambridge: The MIT Press.
Straits Times. (1997). Carving a niche in test wafers.
Teik, L. C. (2000). A Millionaire's tale of guts and glory. *Straits Times*.
Trocki, C. A. (2006). *Singapore: Wealth, power and the culture of control*. Routledge.
Tsui-Auch, L. S. (2003). Learning strategies of small and medium-sized Chinese family firms: A comparative study of two suppliers in Singapore. *Management Learning, 34*(2), 201.
Tsui-Auch, L. S. (2004). The professionally managed family-ruled enterprise: Ethnic Chinese business in Singapore. *Journal of Management Studies, 41*(4), 693–723.

CHAPTER 6

Comparisons and Conclusions

6.1 Political Constraints and the Policy Environment

In this book, I have attempted to explain variation in the economic governance systems linking large structural factors to micro-level decisions. The typological framework I employed examined the interaction between levels of systemic vulnerability faced by governments on the one hand and the number of veto players on the other. I hypothesized that states without the institutionalized constraints embodied in multiple veto player governments will only develop the broadly targeted policy environment necessary for coordinative economic governance institutions when sufficiently high levels of vulnerability offer an alternative form of constraint. Additionally, I hypothesized that states with excessive veto player governments would be unable to overcome the tendency toward the sorts of particularistic policies that lead to hierarchical economic governance institutions, regardless of the level of vulnerability.

Do the interactions between the number of veto players in government and levels of systemic vulnerability have an impact on the policy environment? I hypothesized that increasing levels of external threat, sensitivity to unrest, and resource scarcity will constrain actors in single veto player governments from either offering particularistic policies or radical policy changes.

These hypotheses played out as expected in the within-country comparisons described in the chapters above. The three periods in Thailand

J.D. Moore, *Varieties of Capitalism in Southeast Asia*, The Political Economy of East Asia, DOI 10.1007/978-3-319-53700-9_6

Veto Players		Vulnerability								
		Low			Medium			High		
		Predicted	Case	Observed in Case	Predicted	Case	Observed in Case	Predicted	Case	Observed in Case
One		Particularistic, moderately stable	Post 1969 (MY)	Particularistic, moderately stable	Mixed	Military Rule (TH)	Mixed	Broadly-Targeted	Penang (MY)	Broadly Targeted, Stable
			Single Party (TH)	Particularistic, moderately stable**		Semi-Democracy (TH)	Mixed		Singapore	Broadly Targeted, Stable
			-	-		Pre 1969 (MY)	Broadly Targeted, Stable		-	-
Many		Particularistic, moderately stable	Coalitional Government (TH)	Particularistic, moderately stable	Particularistic, moderately stable	Post-Crisis (TH)	Particularistic, moderately stable	-	Instability Period (TH)*	Particularistic, unstable

Fig. 6.1 Expectations and findings for the policy environment

with single veto player governments conformed to my expectations. In the Military Rule period, moderate levels of vulnerability limited the scale of particularistic policies that the Sarit and Thanom governments were willing to pursue. In the Semi-Democracy period, moderate vulnerability levels likewise caused the government to restrict the scale of particularistic policies to only sectoral matters and with a limited budget. Early in the Single Party period, the Thaksin government experienced moderate vulnerability and limited the degree of particularism, but gradually offered more narrowly targeted policy benefits as vulnerability levels went down. In Malaysia before 1969, the single veto player Alliance government faced moderate vulnerability levels but managed to produce a policy environment more broadly targeted than anticipated by this framework. In Malaysia after 1969, the UMNO-dominated single veto player government faced low vulnerability levels and had a highly particularistic policy environment. High vulnerability levels in Singapore and Penang, by contrast, led to a broadly targeted policy environment.

The framework thus explains the nature of the policy environment in each of the single veto player observations aside from Malaysia immediately after independence. The failure of the framework to explain this case may be due to the fact that the bulk of government spending, where any particularism would be apparent, was funneled at agricultural projects that targeted rural Malays. Additionally, Chinese elites were content with their dominance of the commercial and nascent manufacturing sectors and hesitant to exacerbate inter-communal tensions by pursuing additional state support. I also hypothesized that excessive veto player governments would produce particularistic policy environments, regardless of the degree of vulnerability. As expected, the policy environment in Thailand was particularistic during both the Coalition Government and Post-Crisis periods, despite higher levels of vulnerability in the latter period. The coalitional dynamic substantially undermined efforts to reign in policy particularism (Fig. 6.1).

6.2 The Policy Environment and Capitalist Institutions

Does the policy environment determine the types of economic governance institutions that emerge? I hypothesized that stable, broadly targeted policy environments would facilitate the development of coordinative economic governance institutions because, without the risks produced by radical policy change or the allure of particularistic policy benefits, actors would seek to reduce transaction costs by investing in co-specific assets. Conversely, I expected particularistic policy environments to result in hierarchical economic governance institutions. For corporate governance institutions, the results mostly support the theory.

The mixed policy environment of Thailand's Military Rule period resulted in primarily hierarchical governance institutions. The Semi-Democracy period, which also had a mixed policy environment, was also predominantly hierarchical but saw the development of new, more coordinative structures of corporate governance in the electrical and electronics industry. Likewise, some initial steps were made toward more coordinative structures in the early Single Party Rule period but they faltered as the policy environment became more particularistic. The Post-Independence period in Malaysia, which featured a more broadly targeted policy environment than anticipated by the framework, featured mostly hierarchical corporate governance institutions though the liberal institutions established under the British remained strong. This is more fitting with the original expectation based on a moderate vulnerability and one veto player. Still, however, the typological framework's explanation of this case is the weakest in the study. After 1969 in Malaysia, hierarchical corporate governance institutions thrived as expected under the increasing particularism of the policy environment. In Penang, the state government offered a broadly targeted policy environment but the corporate structures that resulted were something of a hybrid, incorporating some elements of hierarchical and some elements of coordinative governance institutions. The same was true for broadly targeted Singapore. I consider this pattern in greater detail in the section on Chinese-style capitalism below.

For inter-firm linkage institutions, the results also mostly supported the theory. In Thailand, the most strongly coordinative institutions developed during the Semi-Democracy period, with its mixed policy environment. Some coordination occurred during the Military Rule period in the banking and agricultural industries but were absent from manufacturing sector. Some early signs of stronger coordination emerged in the early Single Party Government period but they withered as particularism increased throughout the Thaksin regime. Institutions were hierarchical in the Instability, Coalitional Government, or Post-Crisis periods. Inter-firm linkage institutions were hierarchical in Malaysia before 1969, despite a predictable, broadly targeted policy environment.

After 1969, the institutions remained hierarchical as the policy environment became more clearly particularistic. In Penang and Singapore, the broadly targeted policy environments meant that institutions were highly coordinative.

6.3 Alternative Arguments

Sino Capitalism

Does the modified VoC framework do a better job of explaining the cases than the assumption of an Asian, Confucian, or Chinese model of capitalism? I have observed significant variation in the type of economic governance institutions in the three economies I have studied—even though each is economically dominated by ethnically Chinese actors. The economies most clearly dominated by ethnic Chinese are Singapore, Malaysia before 1969, and Penang; these have not had uniform governance institutions. I can thus reject the proposition that having a strong Chinese influence on the economy is sufficient to produce any uniformly Chinese set of economic governance institutions.

The mechanism proposed in this literature, specific Chinese and Confucian values, also does not produce a specific style of economic governance among Chinese in the countries studied. If it is true that Confucian and ethnic Chinese values lead to a particular style of economic governance, we ought to expect Chinese firms in Penang and the rest of Malaysia to be structured in relatively similar ways and have similar sorts of inter-firm ties. As the Malaysia chapter indicates, this is clearly not the case as Chinese firms in Penang tend to be much more coordinative while those in the rest of the country are more hierarchical. Similarly, Sino-Thai firms have been mostly hierarchical diversified conglomerates while Singaporean Chinese firms have been coordinated. It is clear, however, that firms in the cases studied in this book tended to retain family ownership to a greater degree than expected. In Singapore and Penang particularly, where the model predicted highly coordinated firms, though family firms were not diversified conglomerates, successful firms did not seem to develop cross-shareholding structures or rely on patient capital in the form of large financial institutions. While it is possible that these economies will move in this direction, nothing in these cases suggests that such a trend is occurring. Rather, it may be that just as Japanese and Korean coordinative forms of corporate governance differ from Western European forms, those forms that are developing in these economies are different still. The attributes of finance that are suggested by the VoC argument are long time horizons and reliance on non-public information such as network reputational monitoring.

A coordinative system of corporate governance that emerges out of (and remains distinct to) a hierarchical Chinese family-based system may indeed have an alternative institutional structure. What makes it coordinative is the degree to which financing decisions are (1) long-term, (2) not primarily conditional on price and short-term profitability, and (3) make use of economies of scale and/or scope (i.e. not of the loose diversified conglomerate structure). One segment of the literature on Chinese capitalism seems to be moving in this direction, noting that the Chinese family firm seems to be taking different forms in different institutional context.[1] Further work marrying this literature and the approach applied in this book seems warranted.

Multiethnic Countries

Do ethnic divisions within society preclude economy-wide collaboration embodied in coordinative governance institutions? The cases observed in this study suggest that ethnic homogeneity is not necessary for coordinative governance. Though most successful firms in Penang are owned by ethnic Chinese, there are many successful Malay firms, such as AKN Technology, that play an active role in the dense inter-firm linkages in the state (Bernama Daily Malaysian News 2003; The Edge (Malaysia) 1998; Emmanuel 1998; Ho 2000). In addition, Singapore has also managed to develop collaborative institutions despite ethnic heterogeneity.

Multinational Corporations and Local Institutions

Does the entry of multinational corporations (MNCs) and foreign direct investment (FDI) necessarily undermine the coordinative potential of an economy? In none of the cases selected in this study did we see the rise of the professionally managed widely-held corporation. Instead, MNCs and foreign investors largely worked with what was present. In Singapore, MNCs were willing to develop very strong, close relationships with local private and government-linked corporations. Local representatives of MNCs in Penang nurtured local developers while those in the rest of Malaysia were unwilling to invest in relationship-specific investments necessary for coordinative institutions to develop, despite strong incentives to do so provided by the federal government. MNCs demonstrated willingness to work with local firms in close coordination during the Semi-Democratic period but otherwise were content to utilize Thailand's cheap labor without participating in coordinative systems.

Institutional Malleability

Are inter-firm linkage or corporate governance institutions more malleable? Although the complementarity that forms an integral part of the VoC argument implies that each type of economic governance institution works more effectively when another type of institution of the same variety is in place, it is not clear which type should appear first. In Chap. 2 I hypothesized that, because coordinative inter-firm linkage institutions require firms that are willing to engage in cooperative ventures that require a long time to payoff, they are unlikely to develop before coordinative corporate governance institutions. The evidence collected in this study does not support this conclusion. In Singapore and Penang, strong inter-firm linkage institutions developed while family owned and managed firms were the norm. Gradually these firms developed professional management structures but the inter-firm ties were deep well before.

6.4 Implications

This project's typological framework accounted for variation in the selected cases more accurately than various alternative arguments. Political factors shaped the policy environments of the selected cases and governance institutions developed in response to that environment. In each of the cases, efforts were made to mimic foreign governance institutions without addressing the incentives created by the policy environment. In the early 1990s, the Thai government sought to create liberal corporate governance institutions like stock markets. Diversified family conglomerates simply used the new institutions to expand their own financing options without limiting their control over firm operations. In the 1990s, both Thai and Malaysian governments also sought to mimic the coordinative inter-firm linkage institutions of Singapore and Penang. Institutions like the BoI Unit for Linkage Development in Thailand and the Vendor Development Program in Malaysia sought to promote stronger upstream–downstream coordination among local firms and multinationals. Individual firms, facing particularistic policy environments, were unwilling to develop the co-specific assets required to participate in these institutions.

Ritchie (2010) provides a complementary analysis of worker training institutions, a third form of economic governance institution identified by Hall and Soskice (2001). As mentioned in Chap. 2, Ritchie examines the effect of vulnerability on worker training institutions in Thailand during the Coalition Government and Post-Crisis periods, Malaysia after 1969, and Singapore. As predicted by my typological framework, Singapore and Penang have strongly coordinative worker training institutions. Also, parallel to my findings on inter-firm linkage institutions, he finds that political factors undermined Thai and Malaysian efforts to replicate successful coordinative worker training institutions in Singapore and Penang (Ritchie 2010, 161–169).

These findings suggest that domestic and international actors who committed resources to restructuring these governance institutions would have been better served by focusing on improving the policy environment by constraining governments. Of course, the question is then how to establish these constraints. The Thai cases suggest that the presence of democratic institutions is not sufficient to avoid the emergence of HME institutions. The many veto player governments of the Coalitional Governments and Post-Crisis periods were prone to particularism and the development of hierarchical institutions. Reformation of a country's electoral system can help reduce the number of veto players in such cases. The policy implications of systemic vulnerability are, however, substantially less obvious. External threats and domestic unrest are hardly otherwise desirable conditions.

Hicken and Ritchie (2002), Doner et al. (2009) have suggested that single veto player governments can achieve a predictable policy environment by creating consultative institutions. These institutions provide economic actors with a sufficient appreciation of the government's policy preferences to make the policy environment predictable without sacrificing the government's ability to respond decisively to crises and changes in external conditions. Active participation by key economic actors effectively "ties politicians' hands, raises the barriers to rapid policy reversals, and hence bolsters policy credibility" (Doner et al. 2009, 160). Such non-veto participation could raise the costs of pursuing policy shifts sufficiently to dissuade the government from engaging in radical policy shifts. While it is less immediately clear how these consultative institutions would dissuade particularistic policies, it is at least theoretically possible that some set of institutions could sufficiently raise the costs of doing so.

In 2007 the Thai military junta instituted a new constitution with a hybrid electoral system that incorporated elements of the multimember multi-vote and single member district systems. Even as details of the new constitution were being promulgated, groups began a fairly nuanced public debate over the merits of various electoral systems. Ever since, including after subsequent coups, Thai parties have been campaigning for reform.

Whichever reforms succeed, however, the impact of any change in the electoral system is likely to be muted so long as the military and judiciary are free to undermine election results.[2] The implications for future governance institutions, however, are as yet unclear. If regime instability continues, this framework suggests that actors will want to retain flexibility and will favor hierarchical institutions. If a more activist role for the judiciary is better institutionalized, it has the potential to operate as a separate veto player and constrain the behavior of future governments.[3] If electoral reforms are successful and the 1997 system is re-instituted with more robust checks and balances, the VoC framework suggests that the resulting two-party system will result in liberal institutions.

The future of governance in Malaysia is also unclear. Should the ruling party further erode the health of democratic institutions, it is likely that hierarchical governance will continue to predominate. If, however, BN were to open the political system to more competition, Malaysia's electoral system would likely move toward a two party system. The VoC framework suggests that such a system would strengthen liberal market institutions. With Malaysia's relatively developed capital markets, such a governance system has the potential to develop rapidly.

Singapore's coordinative institutions continue to thrive. Local firms are making the transition to establishing their own global brands, and they continue to make substantial innovations at the technological frontier.

Are these findings generalizable beyond the three Southeast Asian countries examined? Since we have rejected the alternative arguments described above, there is less reason to expect that these Southeast Asian cases systematically differ from other developing countries. Thailand, Singapore, and Malaysia have been more open to foreign investment than most developing countries but the literature on globalization indicates that, were this to have an impact, it would lead to more liberal governance or prevent coordinative governance, neither of which was not the case. Thus, the importance of FDI to these economies should not prevent us from making useful generalizations. Likewise, the substantial variation we observe in the economies dominated by ethnically Chinese actors suggests that the Asian-ness of the cases ought not prevent the application of our findings beyond Asia. It is also important to note that the hierarchical governance system was developed by looking at patterns of diversified family business groups in Latin America. I expect diversified family business groupings to be utilized as an important form of corporate governance across the developing world. To be sure, the findings here are only suggestive of relationships that may be at work in other places. Additional data should be gathered on more and more geographically varied countries in order to systematically test whether the framework employed here holds elsewhere.

Another issue area that requires further study is the difference between the impacts of specific state policies and the overall policy environment. The evidence examined in this study indicates that an effort by the state to promote the development of a particular system of economic governance is not sufficient to foster such development. It is, however, unclear whether such a direct policy is necessary to achieve that end. That is, can coordinative institutions develop in a stable, broadly targeted policy environment even where the state does not intervene to promote them? In each of the instances of strong or mixed coordinative governance that was examined here, the state played such a facilitative or coordinating role. The framework developed here suggests that the private actors involved will have a strong incentive to develop these institutions, though they may find the provision of the requisite monitoring and enforcement capabilities more challenging without the state playing a direct role. This is a particularly important question and one worthy of further study. A cross-national, two-stage study could investigate the factors that motivate direct government policy to promote a particular type of economic governance institution, coordinative inter-firm linkages for example, and then test to see whether the policy environment or direct government policy better explains the successful development of those institutions.

I have, up to this point, remained agnostic as to the relative merits of liberal and coordinative economic governance institutions for successful economic development. To be sure, either form seems more favorable than a system made up of hierarchical governance institutions. My own feeling is that coordinative institutions might be more effective in the diffusion and adoption of already discovered technologies. However, since the real challenge for either system is ensuring that the policy environment is free of particularism, reformers are better off focusing on that question and letting new coordinative, liberal, or some other form of governance institution emerge organically in response to the new policy environment.

Additionally, it is unclear where there is a critical threshold for systemic vulnerability. Because the theory relies on three separate factors (external threat, natural resources, and sensitivity to unrest), it is difficult to pinpoint exactly when a country has 'enough' vulnerability to constrain its leaders from pursuing particularistic policies. Exactly how powerful and belligerent must neighboring countries be before leaders will feel threatened? Will an increase in external threat have as much of an impact as a decline in resource revenues? Are the effects of each of these elements additive, where the effect increases linearly as threat or sensitivity levels are increased? Or are the effects multiplicative, where the marginal impact of an increase in sensitivity is higher when the threat is also high? Unfortunately, neither the theory nor the findings of this project provide much insight into these questions. Ritchie's efforts to compile cross-national data on vulnerability will help to answer to these questions.[4] By carefully structuring statistical analyses of such cross-national data we can parse out these effects and get a better idea of how these three elements interact. Alternatively, a series of controlled comparisons could be done to see whether countries with differing levels of one element respond to a change in another. For instance, we could see how otherwise similar countries with differing levels of external threat respond to a regional or global economic crisis.

This study has used a modified version of the VoC argument to account for variation in economic governance institutions in three Southeast Asian countries. I have incorporated insights from the developmental state literature and Schneider's hierarchical category of economic governance institutions to create a typological framework. In doing so I have expanded the application of the VoC argument beyond the advanced industrialized countries from which it was induced and accounted for gaps in the theory related to single veto player and many veto player governments. The framework's initial success in accounting for the evolution of economic governance institutions in these cases suggests that a cross-national testing is warranted.

Notes

1. For example, see (Zhang and Ma 2009; Yeung, n.d.; Redding 1996; Redding and Witt 2007).
2. TRT's successor party was able to form a government following the first elections under the 2007 constitution but was disbanded by the courts, had its sitting PM removed from power by the courts (for hosting a cooking television program), and lost power after the military put pressure on other parties to form a coalition with the Democrat Party.
3. It is not clear yet whether the judiciary has separate preferences or they are simply representing the interests of other forces in and out of government.
4. Ritchie (2010).

References

Bernama Daily Malaysian News. (2003). AKN Eyes Bigger Market in Asia-Pacific After Acquisition Exercise.

Doner, R. F., Hicken, A., & Ritchie, B. (2009). Political challenges of innovation in the developing world. *Review of Policy Research, 26*(1–2), 151–171.

The Edge (Malaysia). (1998). Net Value—Niche Tech Supplier for MNCs Gets Ready for KLSE.

Emmanuel, M. (1998). AKN Technology to Boost Share. *The New Straits Times.*

Hall, P., & Soskice, D. (2001). *Varieties of capitalism: The institutional foundations of comparative advantage.* Oxford: Oxford University Press.

Hicken, A., & Ritchie, B. (2002). *The origin of credibility enhancing institutions in Southeast Asia.* Paper delivered at the American Political Science annual meeting, 2002.

Ho, J. (2000). New CEO and Acquisitions Should Augur Well for AKN, say Market Observers. *The Edge (Malaysia).*

Redding, S. G. (1996). The distinct nature of Chinese capitalism. *The Pacific Review, 9*(3), 426–441. doi:10.1080/09512749608719195.

Redding, G., & Witt, M. (2007). *The future of Chinese capitalism: Choices and chances.* Oxford: Oxford University Press.

Ritchie, B. (2010). *Systemic vulnerability and sustainable economic growth: Skills and upgrading in Southeast Asia.* Cheltenham: Edward Elgar.

Yeung, H. W. (n.d.). Change and continuity in Southeast Asian Ethnic Chinese business. http://doi.org/10.1007/s10490-006-9007-2.

Zhang, J., & Ma, H. (2009). Adoption of professional management in Chinese family business: A multilevel analysis of impetuses and impediments. *Asia Pacific Journal of Management, 26*(1), 119–139.

Bibliography

Debt Restructuring: Kulthorn Kirby Plan Accepted. (1999, December 1). *Bangkok Post.*
UNITED NATIONS. (2003). UN comtrade database. http://comtrade.un.org/.

J.D. Moore, *Varieties of Capitalism in Southeast Asia*, The Political Economy of East Asia, DOI 10.1007/978-3-319-53700-9

Index

A
Abdul Rahman, Tunku, 108
Advanced Systems Automation (ASA), 154
Air Conditioning and Refrigeration Club, 64
Alliance, 105
Alphatec, 1
Amatayakul, Sompop, 80
Association of Thai industries, 52

B
Badawi, Abdullah, 123
Bangkok International Banking Facilities (BIBF), 73
Bank of Thailand (BoT), 51
Banks, 41
Barisan Nasional (BN), 106
Board of Investment (BoI), 38
BoI Unit for Linkage Development (BUILD), 75
British, 107
Bumiputra, 120

C
Central Provident Fund, 153
Chart Pattana, 71
Chart Thai, 69
Chinese, 41
Choonhavan, Chatichai, 69
Corporate governance institutions, 39
Co-specific assets, 4
Crown Property Bureau, 81

D
Democratic Action Party, 133
Democrat Party, 69

E
Economic Development Board (EDB), 154
Electrical and Electronic Product Club (EEPC), 62, 64
Ekapatanapanich, Saengchai, 85
Eng Hardware, 2

J.D. Moore, *Varieties of Capitalism in Southeast Asia*, The Political Economy of East Asia, DOI 10.1007/978-3-319-53700-9

Excessive Veto Players (EVP), 6, 12, 15, 17, 19, 26, 33, 48–50, 55, 56, 67, 68, 70, 78, 80, 92
Eu, Lim Chong, 135

F
Family business, 39
Federation of Malaysian Manufacturers, 128
Federation of Thai Industries (FTI), 64
Financial Sector Master Plan, 88

G
Gerakan, 133
Gerrymandering, 110

H
Hamzah, Razaleigh, 117
Hin, T.H., 140

I
Ibrahim, Anwar, 120
Industrial Restructuring Plan, 84
Institute of Microelectronics (IME), 157
Inter-firm linkage institutions, 42
Internal Security Act, 133

J
Joint Public Private Consultative Committee, 58

K
Kamol Sukosol group, 53
Kang Young Electric, 44
Kittikachorn, Thanom, 35
Konfrontasi, 107
Kulthorn Kirby, 1, 62

L
Lee, H.S., 109
Leekpai, Chuan, 70
LKT Engineering, 2
Local Industrial Upgrading Programme (LUIP), 156

M
Macroeconomic policy, 28
Mahajak group, 64
Malayan Communist Party (MCP), 107
Malaysia Electric Corporation (MEC), 130
Malaysian Chinese Association (MCA), 105
Malaysian Electrical and Electronics Industry Group (MEEIG), 131
Malaysian Indian Congress (MIC), 109
Malaysian Industry-Government Group for High Technology (MIGHT), 129
Manufacturing Integration Technology (MIT), 155
Marakanond, Rerngchai, 71
Matsushita Electric Company, 114
May 13th, 133

Microfits and methods, 154
Ministry of Finance, 54
Ministry of International Trade and Industry (MITI), 129
Mohamad, Mahathir, 118
Mohamed, Mustapa, 132

N
Nakornthon Bank, 75
National Economic and Social Development Board (NESDB), 57
National Electronics and Computer Technology Center (NECTEC), 64
National Electronics Institute (NEI), 85
National Investment Company (NIC), 112
National Thai, 44
New Aspiration Party (NAP), 86
New Economic Policy (NEP), 120
Nimmanhaeminda, Tarrin, 70

O
OYL, 130

P
Panitchpakdi, Supachai, 70
Panyarachun, Anand, 70
PAS, 134
Penang, 106
Penang Development Corporation (PDC), 136
Pensonic, 139
People's Action Party (PAP), 108
Petronas, 115
Publicly listed firms, 60

R
Ramangkura, Virabongsa, 69
Rojanastien, Boonchu, 53

S
Sabhavasu, Pramual, 69
Sanyo Universal Electric (SUE), 44
Sapura, 131
Sectoral policy, 29
Shinawatra, Thaksin, 86
Siam Cement Group (SCG), 62
Siam Commercial Bank (SCB), 81
Siew Sin, Tan, 109
Silpa-archa, Banharn, 69
Stock Exchange of Thailand (SET), 59
Supinit, Vijit, 70

T
Tanin Industrial, 46
Tan, Vincent, 117
Tinsulanonda, Prem, 54
Thai Chamber of Commerce, 60
Thai CRT, 62
Thai Rak Thai (TRT), 86
Thai Toshiba Electric, 44
Thammasak, Sanya, 47
Thananchanan, Chavlit, 69
Thanarat, Sarit, 35

U
Ungphakorn, Puey, 35
Unimech, 140

United Malays National Organization
(UMNO), 105

V

Varieties of capitalism, 3
  coordinated market economies, 3
  hierarchical market economy, 7, 10
  liberal market economies, 3
Vendor Development Program, 131
Veto players, 4
  excessive veto players, 6
Virawan, Amnuay, 70
Vision 2020, 122

Y

Yew, Lee Kuan, 150

Z

Zainuddin, Daim, 117